PRA

"What a marvelous and fruitful collision of the scientific, poetic, and contemplative temperaments, all in one author and one book. For those who dream of the recovery in our late modern age of an 'integrated vision' of things, uniting natural philosophy and speculative wisdom and spiritual curiosity, Martin Nowak's *Beyond* is like a reassuring lantern suddenly shining out along a dark path late at night."
—**DAVID BENTLEY HART**, author of *Roland in Moonlight* and *All Things Are Full of Gods: The Mysteries of Mind and Life* (forthcoming)

"Martin Nowak's remarkable text *Beyond* is impossible to categorize as a literary genre. Part romantic tone poem, part Socratic dialogue, part biblical Wisdom literature, part primer in contemporary scientific theory, it takes the reader on a journey into ultimate questions which is as poetically rich as it is astonishing. Anyone who has ever wondered about the origins and meaning of the universe must read this book and reflect upon the depth of scientific and theological mysteries it evokes: it is the reader who is challenged, and who cannot remain unchanged by the lure of the narrative."
—**SARAH COAKLEY**, Norris-Hulse Professor of Divinity, emerita, University of Cambridge

"*Beyond* is a devotional meditation on God and Love, more poetry than prose, by evolutionary biologist Martin Nowak. His is a Platonic universe where mathematics and truth are the ultimate reality. The meditation moves from Plato to Augustine and Aquinas, to Krishna, Siddhartha, and the Tao. It is an extended dialogue between a male Faustian voice and a mysterious female presence, an unnamed Beatrice, who may well be divine and becomes his guide to leave the cave of shadows."
—**DAVID HAIG**, Professor of Organismic and Evolutionary Biology, Harvard University

"If there ever could be a sequel to both Hermann Hesse's *Siddhartha* and Umberto Eco's *The Name of the Rose*, Martin Nowak's *Beyond* would be it. The harvest of a lifetime of thinking about religion,

science, and their explanations of the world, this book takes the reader on a Socratic journey of infinite discoveries. It is a page-turner to be read and re-read."
—WINRICH FREIWALD, Denise & Eugene Chinery Professor of Neuroscience and Behavior, Rockefeller University

"Martin Nowak's *Beyond* is an engaging fusion of science, philosophy, meditative prayer, love story, and mystery. It can be seen as a poetic version of *Sophie's World* for adults. Its spirituality is unique. You will be thinking, guessing, and smiling until the last page!"
—KAMILA NAXEROVA, Assistant Professor of Genetics, Harvard Medical School

"The most powerful superstition of the modern age was that certain and useful knowledge could be seized by man, would he simply surrender his urgent yearning for the gift of wisdom that springs from the center of his being. But superstition it was indeed, as Martin Nowak shows in this long meditation, at once treatise and poem, Socratic dialogue and lyric meditation. Increasingly, those who study the philosophy of science have concluded that positive knowledge is only possible and desirable when restored to its ancient foundation in the love of wisdom and the even more profound yearning for the *logos* of the divine. Nowak was there before most others, and is here now, to draw us into the life of the *logos* through this series of rhapsodic explorations. The truth is One, he shows us, and it is calling us to communion, even now in the concrete hospital ward of our lives."
—JAMES MATTHEW WILSON, Cullen Foundation Chair of English Literature, University of Saint Thomas

"*Beyond* is a moving reflection, in poetic form, on fundamental truths in theology, philosophy, mathematics, and the natural sciences. Here, Martin Nowak recovers an ancient tradition—going back to Plato, Augustine, Boethius, and Dante, but now lost to the academic world—of conveying the beauty of its content by its own beautiful form. The book will speak powerfully to readers with or without prior knowledge of its themes."
—JOSEPH LAPORTE, Professor of Philosophy, Hope College

"Martin Nowak's *Beyond* may be one of the most idiosyncratic, original, and marvelous works of poetry I have read in a very long time. Astonishment inhabits every line. I came away from it in a state of wonder."
—**MICHAEL MARTIN**, Director, Center for Sophiological Studies; Editor, *Jesus the Imagination*

"In precise, almost haunting language, a world-leading mathematician attempts to help his readers find God. From Buddha to Borges, from evolutionary dynamics to the irrational number π, Martin Nowak's poetic quest for truth is a radiant distillation of philosophy and science, a journey sparkling with insight. And also a love story, bursting with passion for beauty, and a cry against selfishness, and for goodness. Whatever their conception of God may be, readers brave enough to open their minds and hearts will not fail to be moved."
—**OREN HARMAN**, author of *The Price of Altruism* and *Evolutions: Fifteen Myths That Explain Our World*

"*Beyond* is an awe-filled contemplation of some of the greatest questions science, religion and philosophy can ask."
—**GABRIELA LOBINSKA**, Weizmann Institute of Science

BEYOND

BEYOND

BY MARTIN NOWAK

Angelico Press

First published in the USA
by Angelico Press 2024
Copyright © by Martin Nowak 2024

All rights reserved:
No part of this book may be reproduced
or transmitted, in any form or by
any means, without permission

For information, address:
Angelico Press, Ltd.
169 Monitor St.
Brooklyn, NY 11222
www.angelicopress.com

ppr 979-8-89280-017-4
cloth 979-8-89280-018-1
ebook 979-8-89280-019-8

Book and cover design
by Michael Schrauzer

CONTENTS

Movement 1   3
Movement 2   87
Movement 3   181
Movement 4   267
Movement 5   333
Movement 6   355

Endnotes   387

beyond
the veil
of confusion
of selfishness
lies another world
a world that is very different
a world where light travels freely

MOVEMENT I

1

they walked uphill through vineyards
immersed in musings over philosophy

they had met a few days before

she was curious asking many questions
they were natural, childlike and deep
so were his answers

spring had just started and the world
had a new meaning in her presence

when they reached the top of the hill
they sat down in the grass
which was warm and dry

in front of them was a small town
behind it a river with forests
hills were rolling in the distance

the two medieval towers of a
monastery pointed to heaven

what is truth? she asked

do you mean "logos"?

i mean "truth"

her eyes were penetrating
as if she could see into his soul
he did not hold her gaze for long
he looked elsewhere

he noticed the stillness of the trees
the gentle unfolding of the clouds

the world is whatever is the case

truth is often taken for granted
we think we know what it means
that something can be true or false

a mathematical expression
can be true or false
it is harder to understand truth
outside of mathematics

but it seems that also verbal
statements can be true or false
"Socrates was a man"

yet i think anything that can be true
or false is a mathematical statement

Socrates is an element in a set
the set of all men

what is a set? she asked

do you mean in mathematical glory
or in a simple every day sense?

every day simplicity suffices for me
she said quickly

a set is a collection of things
some things belong to it
while others do not

the set of animals, of plants
the set of days in a week
the set of people in a town
the set of even numbers
the set of odd numbers
the set of perfect numbers

...there again the quest for perfection

the set of prime numbers
the set of Platonic forms
—i meant to say Platonic solids
he corrected himself—
the set of Platonic solids

sets can contain other sets

Movement 1

she looked at him
it never goes without math
it doesn't

he was aware of insects and birds
the smell of flowers and of trees
he inhaled the warm air of spring

they were quite alone
if there were other people
they were at a distance

he thought of that letter written long ago

wenn die ganze Welt um mich her
in meiner Seele ruht...[1]

truth is in poetry... his mind wandered
then tell me about logos, she said

logos has a threefold meaning
the fundamental truth about everything
the wisdom to conceive this truth
the words to describe this wisdom

Plato's great idea is
that the world makes sense
that we can discover this sense
that searching for this sense
is the purpose of life

it is beautiful and simple

already at the time of Plato there were
skeptics who denied this world view
one of them was Gorgias

Gorgias, the skeptic
waged a threefold denial:
there is no fundamental truth
if there was a fundamental truth
there is no wisdom to conceive it
if there was such a wisdom
there are no words to describe it

Gorgias was a skilled orator
rich from giving speeches
and from teaching students
he commissioned a life-sized
statue of himself in pure gold

i guess we are siding with Plato
she offered with a smile

let us side with Plato

he looked toward the hills
on the other side of the valley
the city was behind them

but in the modern world
many people side with Gorgias

there are no absolutes
everything is relative
there are mere opinions

in the end of this path
only nihilism is left
words have no meaning
they are expressions
of power over others
manipulative tools

but if you want to go there then
why bother to be a philosopher
or a scientist or mathematician?

in this place of denial what is
the activity of doing science?

instead Plato proposed that meaning
emanates from eternal forms

here in this world we live in a cave
we only see shadows of the forms

light from outside projects
the shadows of the forms
on the wall of the cave

Movement 1

here inside the cave
he made a sweeping gesture
pointing at everything around them
we only see those dancing shadows

philosophy, the love of wisdom
is an activity that leads us out
of the cave into the dazzling light

am i a shadow inside the cave?
she wondered

if you are confronted with truth
you cannot look into her eyes
he thought

the sunlight was now fully on them
they were in need of some shade

a collection of small trees was nearby
with pristine leaves and new blossoms
birds explored them for nesting sites

was she leading him out of the cave?

if all of this is just the interior of the
cave then where are those forms?
she asked

if you are a realist, like Plato, the forms
have a real existence in underlying reality

Aristotle, Plato's greatest student, denied
the independent existence of the forms

he argued that you have to derive
them from the material world
this proposition makes Aristotle
an empiricist as opposed to a realist

if every red object in the universe
were to disappear the form red
could not be known or would not
even exist according to Aristotle

i think i am a realist, he added
he was amused by this term
and by the idea that someone
could consider him a realist

how do you derive the form of
the good from the material world?
she asked

i do not know, he answered
i am a realist

if Aristotle says we need to
derive the forms empirically
then how does Plato think
we could know the forms?

both for Plato and for Aristotle
intuitive understanding of the forms
is the highest kind of knowledge

Plato argued that we know the forms
from a previous life in heaven

there is something in us which we
know but which cannot be learned
hence Plato's recall to memory

Plato believed in multiple lives
and in heaven, she repeated

i love those ideas, she thought
they give me a sensation as if
remembering from a previous life

she said, memories of a previous life
how beautiful! sometimes it does feel
to me as if i had such memories

what did Plato think about God?
she asked

he introduced God as form of the Good
as a perfect being, as a maker of all

Movement 1

these ideas were further developed
by Aristotle who described God
as unmoved mover, as primary cause

both of them thought that everything
which moves is caused to be moved
by something else

in this chain is no infinite regress
thus we must arrive at a first mover
who is unmoved or who moves itself

there could be multiple first movers
she interjected, in principle

of course! but our quest is not done
until we arrive at the One

the One? she asked

if there are two principles
governing the world we ask
what do they have in common?

do you agree?—probably

also "moving" here is more
than mere physical motion
fire can move wood to burn
a thought can move you
to do good in the world
or a prayer…

…move not, dear saint

they were silent

and what is regress?

there can be infinite progress:
each number is followed by a larger one
positive integers go to plus infinity
each number is preceded by a smaller one
negative integers go to minus infinity

but there cannot be infinite regress
you cannot have 2 without 1—do you agree?

it makes sense to say there is no 2 without 1
but does this argument lead to God, the One?

he was silent

i am not sure what to make of this
she answered, not yet anyway

sometimes i am not sure either, he said

are you sure now?—i am

after some time he continued

Plato's forms point toward God
especially the form of the Good
which he associated with God

the form of the Good provides
the light that illuminates the path
which leads us out of the cave

Plato and Aristotle were taken up
by Christianity, Judaism, and Islam
they provided a solid foundation
for how to think about God
inadvertently or by choice
they became makers of religion

you can see that philosophy and
religion joined forces long ago

he paused

what is this form of the Good?
she asked

it is the highest form which
illuminates all other forms
for the reason that it is good
that those other forms exist

Movement 1

poetry! she exclaimed

why not? he replied

the form of the Good and the form
of Beauty are the same form
what is good is also beautiful
what is not good is not beautiful

is this so? she wondered

think of beauty in its truest form
the essence of beauty, not superficial beauty
which can be a deceptive trap for the senses

they were quiet for some time
tracing different lines of thought

he recalled the opening of a Mahler movement
flowers were in bloom and love was innocent
but the world around was no distant memory
instead he was suspended in the moment
which he wanted to last forever—*verweile doch!*[2]

suddenly she said
what prevents you from seeing
absolute beauty is selfish desire
if you distance yourself
from all egotistical motives
you become a force for the good
and this is the same good
which you call beautiful

he looked at her in surprise but was silent

then they continued to walk side by side
she was close to him and came closer each step

she asked again, where are those forms?

he replied, where are the numbers?
the relationships among numbers?
the theorems of mathematics?
the true arithmetic? the eternal laws
of nature instantiated in this world?

after some time he continued
Augustine who was a philosopher
and a teacher of Christianity proposed
that forms are ideas in the mind of God
he found a home for Platonic Ideas

they rested on a wooden bench
overlooking a clearing with a field
on the other side of the valley
were hills covered in forests

then i too exist in the mind of God
she voiced, we all do, he thought

God was ever present to me, she said
when i was a child there was God
i could pray to him and talk to him
he was within me, he was around me

after some time she added, i think
God is more than the form of the Good
if there are other forms God is them too
and their instantiations to an extent

your thoughts are deep, he said

she laughed, i know nothing
i know that i know nothing

they had only water with them
i love the taste of pure water, she said

he realized he was very hungry
the emptiness turned him inside out
it became an offering to her

the world was supremely beautiful
immersed in a deep afternoon light

absolutely nothing was in motion
and even time itself stood still

Movement 1

Plato's teacher was Socrates
Socrates never wrote anything
or at least nothing is preserved

when Plato writes Socrates teaches
he asks questions and gives answers
this is called a Socratic dialogue

the dialogues revolve around forms
but never reach certainty about them
you can approach them in knowledge
but you can never fully reach them

Socratic dialogues end in a state
called "aporia"—out of resource

it was Socrates who said
i know that i know nothing

did he? she asked
are we in a Socratic dialogue?

not if we reach certainty

she laughed

while Socrates never reached
certainty about any of the forms
there are three things which
he proclaimed with certainty

all learning is only remembering
all evil is only ignorance
nothing evil can happen to a good person

do these make sense to you?

we have talked about the first, she said
i think i understand the second

full knowledge of the good prevents
you from committing any evil acts
partial knowledge implies ignorance
which can result in bad choices

after some silence she continued
for unlocking the third statement
i need a key you have not yet provided

was it awe or hunger inverting him?
was it the spring or the emptiness
or the unfolding Mahler movement?

you are right the key is the following
a person is fundamentally her soul
she alone is guardian of her soul

he looked at her—briefly

oh yes, now i understand, she exclaimed
if she is good she will not harm her own soul
others who hurt her body cannot harm her soul
if they hurt her body they harm their own soul

this message may be difficult to grasp
it requires deep love and forgiveness

it was as if something had fallen
into place in the fabric of the universe
or in the human perception thereof

Gnothi seauton, he said, know thyself
a Delphic maxim inscribed in the temple
which Socrates evoked to argue that
the unexamined life is not worth living

have you been in Delphi? he asked her

i have seen the sanctuary—long ago

now their path traversed a forest
the sunlight fell sideways between
the trunks of magnificent trees
which were radiant in gold

they found a place which offered food
let us only drink something, she proposed
for i want you to be hungry

Movement 1

hungry for what? hungry for truth!

they sat down by a table outside
they observed the night closing in

on the way back she said
do you feel the earth turning beneath you?

on a meadow they were under the stars
he pointed to arcturus the bearer of spring

have you held a star in your fingertips?
have you ever ruled a world?

2

in a remote library a breath of life
lifted a sheet from a wooden desk

the paper was of a weightless kind
or gravity was less willing to act on it
since it glided slowly through the air
enabling a bystander to read words
on the page twisting and turning

a wonderful serenity has taken possession of my soul
i am so absorbed in the exquisite sense of tranquil existence
that i neglect my talents—i am incapable of drawing
a single stroke yet i was never a greater artist

while the valley teems with vapor around me
and the meridian sun strikes the upper surface
of the impenetrable foliage of trees
and a few gleams steal into the inner sanctuary
i throw myself down in the tall grass by the stream

as i lie close to earth a thousand plants are noticed by me
when i hear the buzz of the little world among the stalks
and grow familiar with the countless indescribable forms
i feel the presence of the Almighty who formed us in his image
by the breath of universal love which bears and sustains us

and then my friend when heaven and earth dwell in my soul
like the form of a beloved—i think with longing
oh could i describe those visions! could i impress upon paper
what is then in me that it might be the mirror of my soul
as my soul is the mirror of the infinite God!

you succumb to those images—the paper still gliding
never reaching the floor, never finding the ceiling
in that remote limitless library

3

Augustine searching for God
asked the mountains are you God?
they said we are not but he made us
he asked the clouds are you God?
they said we are not but he made us

Augustine's premise was
God created the world

he wondered out of what?
he concluded out of nothing

God made the world *ex nihilo*

he was the first to propose this idea
usually creation is out of something
but for Augustine it is out of nothing

he asked another intriguing question:
what did God do before creating the world?

Augustine concluded: nothing
because only then God created time
before that event there was no time

they had met for another hike
exploring both nature and God
this time they had chosen the hills
immediately north of the city

he had hoped to spend some part
of the Easter weekend with her
and his wish had been granted

walking beside her he contemplated
before i met her there was time
when i am not with her there is time
when i am with her there is no time
what does this make her?

Augustine read in Genesis that
God created the world in six days
he knew six was a perfect number

Augustine opined that those six days
were mentioned for purpose of narrative
rather than to specify a certain time span
because God creates with time not in time

he said, if something in the Bible
is at variance with a scientific fact
the biblical statement should still
be taken literally but spiritually
thereby Augustine laid the foundation
for the dialogue of science and religion

Augustine converted to Christianity
when he was 31 — he was baptized
together with his son Adeodatus
in Milan during Easter Vigil 387

Easter was late this year, he thought
as it had been in 387

of Augustine they say he read so much that
you wonder how he could have written anything
he wrote so much that few could have read it all

he was a master of the Latin language

his *Confessions* are an outpouring declaration
of love for God and a moving account of his life

he mentions in passing how concepts
arose in his mind which we now hold
as foundations of Christian philosophy

for example that evil is not a substance
or that evil is less real than the good

Augustine writes in the *Confessions*

Movement 1

in Thee abide fixed for ever the first causes of
all things unabiding and of all things changeable
the springs abide in Thee unchangeable
and in Thee live the eternal reasons
of all things unreasoning and temporal

he also wrote

Thou awakest us to delight in Thy praise
for Thou madest us for Thyself and our
heart is restless until it reposes in Thee

she repeated
my heart is restless until it reposes in Thee

long ago i learned about Augustine
she said, but i guess i was too young then
to appreciate the extent of his influence

is he shown with a book and a burning heart?

usually with a book signifying he is a scholar
and sometimes with a burning heart because
his love for the Lord consumes him, he replied

i have a burning heart too, she thought

after some reflection she said
i may understand his remark about evil
if God is good then He excludes evil
He makes evil less real than the good

does he also agree with Socrates
that all evil is only ignorance?

Augustine proposed that doing evil
is turning away from a higher level
of goodness toward a lower level

there is a graduation of goodness
evil is the absence of goodness
it does not exist in the same way
as the good exists

the city was now in full view
they saw the bridges over
the stream that divided it
the towers of many churches
and some new tall buildings

would you like to go to church with me?
she suddenly asked, to the Easter vigil?

it is the wish of my heart, he answered

we will find one that begins at midnight
and ends at sunrise as in the old days

we can talk for a long time until it starts
you can tell me more about Christianity
and all that i should have learned long ago
or better remembered from previous lives

from your previous life in heaven?

oh don't count on that, she said
who knows where i am from

he laughed and said
i have some superficial knowledge
but you have embracing wisdom
i know words but you know forms
i am a student, you are a teacher

is there anything else you wish
to add? she asked

she thought, what made him say this?
he wondered, why did i say this?

according to a legend Augustine once
encountered a boy on the seashore
the boy had made a hole in the sand
and was pouring sea water into the hole

what are you doing? asked Augustine
i am pouring the entire sea into this hole
but this is impossible! said Augustine

Movement 1

and you want to understand God?
the boy retorted and was gone

after some recollection he said
this hymn is from Augustine too

Late have i loved you
o beauty ever ancient ever new
late have i loved you
you were within me but i was outside
it was there that i searched for you

in my unloveliness i plunged into
the lovely things which you created
you were with me but i was not with you

created things kept me from you
yet if they had not been in you
they would have not been at all

you called, you shouted
you overcame my deafness
you flashed, you shone
you dispelled my blindness
you breathed your fragrance on me

i drew in breath now i pant for you
i have tasted you now i hunger
and thirst for more you touched me
and i burned for your peace

again these words moved her

am i speaking to God as Augustine did
or am i speaking to her? he wondered

they were looking over the great city
he thought how few of its people
were at the moment reflecting words
Augustine had taught us long ago

Augustine studied greek philosophers
he liked Plato's approach which gave
him tools to think about the world

he admired the concept that
philosophy was a practice enabling
people to lead a life worth living

he faulted them for only one aspect
the Platonists thought they could
reach their goal of their own effort

for Augustine it is clear that nothing
can be achieved without God's help

Augustine asked why is it given
to some people to believe in God?
he concluded that even faith is a gift
which comes from the grace of God

does that make you happy or sad?

it makes me happy, she replied

it made Thomas Aquinas happy too

i have spoken too quickly, she interrupted
it makes me sad that some people think
they do not believe in God but it makes
me happy that faith or love for God
originates as a gift that comes from God

God who loves all people uniformly
allows a diversity of perspectives
in this temporal unfolding, she added

these varying worldviews are preliminary
given the fragmented knowledge we have

is Augustine's view preliminary? he asked

of course, she replied, although very blessed

they had reached the shadow of tall trees

Movement 1

Aquinas was another great philosopher
some say he was the greatest of all times
others object but might still concede
that he was the greatest philosopher
between Aristotle and Descartes
which amounts to two thousand years

as a child he asked his teacher a question

what is God? she interrupted

how did you know?

what else should a child ask?

in any case the teacher could not
answer his question and therefore
Aquinas became a theologian

between the trees they found a place
to look at the city—they sat down

once Aquinas was on a hill and someone
pointed to the valley before them and said
how amazing would it be to own this land

Aquinas answered instead he would prefer
the missing page in Aristotle's manuscript

what you own outside has finite value
what you own inside has infinite value
what has infinite value outside of you
you cannot own, she said

after a brief silence she added
all finite values collapse before God
they come to nothing

where are you from? he wondered

Aquinas made the argument that
both faith and reason bring us to God
faith is an easier path for many people
but reason gets us there eventually

he said every argument against Christianity
can be shown wrong based on reason alone
thus the engagement with God is rational

i love this concept, she said

centuries later the church followed up thus:
God's existence can be known with certainty
from the created world by light of human reason

i believe the statement to be true
yet i have never convinced my friends
who question God's existence

words do not convince, she said, lives do

he was silent then proceeded with words

Aquinas examined the question
whether God exists

whenever he contemplated a question
he listed all arguments for and against
sometimes he gave many objections

but against the existence of God
he found only two arguments
over time these were the only two
that were made in one way or another

the first objection is called
the philosopher's argument

God is infinitely good
God is all knowing
God is all powerful
yet there is evil in the world

since there is evil in the world
God cannot be infinitely good
or He cannot be all knowing
or He cannot be all powerful

Movement 1

one way to resolve it, she proposed
would be to go back to Augustine
who argued evil is less real than good

there is a gradient of goodness
ignorance lets you choose
a lesser good instead of a greater one
ignorance is distance from God

does this resolve the contradiction?

yes i think so, he said
this is a very good argument
did you just come up with it?

how could i answer that question
if all learning is only remembering?

Aquinas also replied to the objection
using Augustine but differently, he said

Aquinas states the objection succinctly:
if one of two contraries is infinite
the other must be excluded
since God implies infinite goodness
evil cannot be discoverable in the world
but evil is discoverable and therefore—
it seems—God does not exist

Aquinas then cites Augustine:
since God is the highest good He would
not allow any evil to exist in His works
unless His omnipotence and goodness
were such as to bring good out of evil

then Aquinas adds: it is part
of the infinite goodness of God
that He should allow evil to exist
and out of it produce the good

yesterday was Good Friday, she said
which is a primary example of the idea

Aquinas's second argument against
the existence of God is what is now
called the scientist's argument:

it seems that everything in the world
can be explained by other principles
supposing God did not exist and
thus it is superfluous to evoke God

scientists might think there is no need
for God since the universe runs by itself
propelled along by the forces of nature

abruptly she got up and said
let us gain the ridge to enjoy
the sunlight for a bit longer
they ascended in silence

she thought, can one really account for
everything supposing God did not exist?
is God not present in every person?
in every pair of eyes that looks at me?
in the unfolding promise of every day?
in each moment whether joyful or sad?
is God not existence in all that exists?
beginning, middle, and end of all life?
is God in the taste of pure water
and in the emptiness of empty space?
is the world not moved by the Divine?
are mountains and rock faces not
coronated by those holy shadows?

was she lovesick for God?
was God her first thought?
her ultimate eternal desire?
her one and only dream?

after some time he continued

Aquinas's answer to the scientist's objection
is that everything done by nature must be
traced back to God, everything done by
human will must be traced back to God

Movement 1

Aquinas differentiates between processes
caused by human choice and processes
caused by principles of nature but neither
of them could occur without God

Aquinas then proceeds with the five ways
for thinking about the existence of God
he does call them proofs although they
are not proofs in a mathematical sense
they leave us with lingering uncertainty

in a state out of resource? she asked

probably out of resource, he answered

but before Aquinas gives his five ways
he writes "it is said in the person of
God i am who am; *ego sum qui sum*"
again very succinct, very beautiful!

the first way is based on movement
everything that is put in motion
is moved by something else
we follow this chain of movers
to a first unmoved mover
who is put in motion by no other
this first mover we understand to be God

the second way is based on causality
no thing is an efficient cause of itself
because no thing can be prior to itself
we trace this chain of efficient causes
until we arrive at a first efficient cause
to which we give the name God

the third way is based on existence
if everything can cease to exist
there is a state where nothing existed
then nothing would exist now which is absurd
thus there is at least one necessary existent
which we call God

the fourth way uses gradation
there are degrees like good, better, best
the maximum in a category is the cause of it
hence there must be something which is
to all things the cause of their being
goodness and every other perfection
and again this we call God

the fifth way is based on design
as the arrow is aimed by the archer
some intelligent being must exist
by whom all natural things are directed
to their end and this being we call God

God is defined in the five ways
as the unmoved mover
as the first cause
as the necessary being
as the absolute being
as the grand designer

it is worthwhile to add that for Aquinas
movement is more than physical motion
for instance fire moves wood to burn
love moves us to do good in the world

the fifth way seems to fly in the face
of science which holds for certain that
complex structures arise from simple rules
without the need of interfering designers

but probing deeper you find no contradiction
contemplate what is the end of natural things
is there purpose without a giver of purpose?
can you have any purpose without God?
can there be physical forces without God?
can there be biological evolution without God?

and what is an intelligent being?
one that delights in truth
one that loves mathematics
one that holds ideas in its mind

Movement 1

after some silence she said, i need time
to meditate on each of those five ways
in brevity they can be quite perplexing

he laughed, Maimonides wrote a book
entitled "God, a guide for the perplexed"
but if you were not perplexed about God
before reading it you would be afterwards

Maimonides described God as
an infinite ocean of existence
out of whom all things originate
beside Him there is no second
beyond Him there is no other

he added in his thoughts
beside her there is no second
beyond her there is no other

but before you choose to accept
some, all, or none of the five ways
i need to add a few more details

it is a pleasant evening, she noted
it seems as if time stands still or
moves only imperceptibly slowly

does time move by itself or is it
moved by another? he wondered

before Aquinas, before Maimonides
and influencing both of them there was
a great scholar of the islamic golden age

Avicenna was a celebrated polymath
who contributed to every discipline
alchemy, medicine, geography, astronomy
physics, mathematics, theology, poetry

no intended order i guess, she said

Avicenna gave a proof for God's existence
which is called the proof of the truthful

he distinguishes between a thing that needs
an external cause to exist and a thing
that is guaranteed to exist by its essence

he calls the first contingent, the second necessary
he proves there must be a necessary existent

he notes that every contingent thing
needs something other than itself to bring
it into existence which leads to a chain

others argue this chain cannot be infinite
because there is no infinite regress
but Avicenna allows the chain to be infinite

Avicenna says: consider the entire chain
the entire collection of things that exist
that have ever existed or will ever exist

there are two possibilities

first, this collection is contingent
in this case something outside of
the collection causes it to exist
this outside thing cannot be contingent
because then it would be in the collection
thus this outside thing is necessary

second, the collection itself is necessary

in both cases we have a necessary existent

hence Avicenna declares he has proven
that there must be a necessary existent
subsequently he goes on to associate
the necessary existent with God

what do you make of it? he asked

arguments for the existence of God
are all somewhat similar, she said
but this one is the most thorough

Movement 1

before you decide let's go back to Aquinas
his five ways should be seen in light of
preceding material which he presents

in his *Summa Theologiae* he asks the question
if the proposition "God exists" is self-evident

he gives three arguments in favor

first he cites John of Damascus for saying
"knowledge of God is naturally implanted in all"
what is known naturally can be seen as self-evident

second he uses the ontological proof of Anselm:
once the signification of the word God is understood
it is clear that God exists because God signifies
that than which nothing greater can be conceived

that which exists both mentally and actually
is greater than that which exists only mentally
thus as soon as "God'" is understood
it exists mentally and therefore actually

third, Aquinas notes that existence of truth
is self-evident: for whoever denies existence
of truth grants that truth does not exist

if truth does not exist then the proposition
"truth does not exist" is true
but if one thing is true there is truth

Aquinas cites from the gospel of John
"I am the way, the truth and the life"
since God is truth the existence
of God becomes self-evident

is God not more than truth? she wondered

Aquinas takes down the three arguments
he cites "the philosopher" for saying no one
can admit the opposite of what is self-evident
for Aquinas "the philosopher" is Aristotle

Aquinas simply continues with Psalm 52:
"the fool said in his heart there is no God"
therefore the opposite of the proposition
"God exists" can be mentally admitted

by a fool? she exclaimed

and thus "God exists" is not self-evident

this sounds like poetry to me, she said
very beautiful poetry of course

all great philosophy is poetry, he replied

is mathematics poetry, too? she asked

he was silent

if the Easter vigil starts at midnight
what will we do until then? he asked

we will walk and keep warm

what if it gets too dark or too cold?

God will provide, she said

what is happening here? he thought

Aquinas then resolves it all by saying
a thing can be self-evident in two ways
first, self-evident in itself though not to us
second, self-evident in itself and to us

Aquinas proposes that "God exists" is
self-evident in itself but not to us
thus the existence of God should be shown
from effects that are more known to us

"God exists" is self-evident in itself
because the predicate is the subject:
God is His own existence

the essence of God is existence

Movement 1

all created things have existence
which is given to them by God
but God is His own existence

all created things are composite
in their essence and existence

what creatures are and the fact
that they exist is not the same

but for God what He is and the
fact that He is are truly identical

Aquinas says of God
Deus est ipsum esse per se subsistens
God is His own existence
God is His own act of being

for God being is His very essence
created beings are caused by Him
all created beings are His effect

if a thing has being God is present to it
being is innermost in each thing and hence
God is innermost present to each thing

i can rest my case, he was exhausted
he had reached the end of a journey
which archer had guided him?

the sun was very low now
there was peaceful tranquility

she turned to him and said
you have given me enough
information and i am ready
to offer you my own opinion

i admire the philosophers' attempts
toward understanding God
i humbly bow to their wisdom
everyone who is deeply interested
in the world should study their writings

anyone who wants to learn about God
should know their tools and concepts
they lay a foundation for personal search

philosophy as a practice, as a way to lead life
is praiseworthy, it is a good path for many

however i question the notion that
the unexamined life is not worth living
a saint serves God without knowing herself

the sun had just touched the horizon
while they could not see the sunset
because they were enclosed by tall trees
they sensed it; the air was motionless

that all beings, all things have existence
given to them by God but God is his own
existence is a very important insight

i would call it true by definition
true by your choice of how you see
the world and how you think about God

regarding proofs for the existence of God
and you have mentioned several of them
from Plato, Aristotle, Avicenna, Anselm
and five by Aquinas—they are clever

they help us to approach this question
they do not force inescapable conclusions
they do not have the rigor of mathematics

if they had been mathematical proofs
a single one would have been enough
to hold off a plenitude of doubters

a mathematical proof for God's existence
is not conceivable in my opinion
mathematics cannot capture God's essence
mathematics is not above God

mathematical proofs operate within frames
but God exceeds every boundary

Movement 1

the philosopher's five ways are meditations
from the created world to the creator
from effects we can see to their cause

she smiled

maybe Aquinas called Aristotle the philosopher
knowing that in the future someone would call
him, Aquinas, the philosopher—as i have done

for one who loves God
the proofs are good meditations
for one who doubts God
the proofs may help him realize
that meaningful concepts of God
are different from what he rejects

for one who loves God
no proof is necessary
for one who denies God
no proof is possible
—not in the here and now

evidently the world is arranged
for us to have this choice

this choice is given to us by God
this choice defines us
we must live with this choice!

as the philosopher has taught us
the existence of God is evident in itself
but not necessarily to us and hence
we have a choice—the choice is ours
the choice is yours and mine

there is a road i wish everyone to take
because it leads to profound insight
to indescribable beauty and everlasting love

as for the proclamation of the Church which i admire:
God's existence can be known with certainty from
the created world by the light of human reason
i grant this to be true with one small addition
... for a loving heart

as the lover knows his immortal beloved
the loving heart knows God from the created world

moreover this overwhelming love is entirely rational
love is the rational yet burning desire for the good
we wish to stand in proximity of the good forever

she was silent

the sun had gone down beyond the horizon
they were alone under the trees
if there were any sounds around them
they did not perceive them

she said, let us be quiet for some time
in this precious moment after sunset
remember this is the night of all nights
if you like we can pray...

...remove your shoes, he thought
for you are standing on holy ground

he touched the soft forest floor
did he kneel before her? or God?

Lord, forgive me three sins due to my limitation
thou art everywhere but i worship you here
thou art without form but i worship you in her
thou needest no praise but i worship you incessantly

she said

Lord, this is the night when your son who
was fully human passed from death to life

this is the night when our ancestors
moved unharmed through the Red Sea

this is the night when the pillar of fire
destroyed the darkness of sin

this is the night of which it is written
the night shall be bright as a day

Movement 1 39

o truly blessed night
worthy alone to know the time and hour
when Christ rose from the underworld

o truly blessed night
when heaven is wed to earth

Lord you have incited my love
may this light burn undimmed
to overcome any darkness

may this flame be found still
burning by the morning star
the one and true morning star
which never sets

they were silent
he wished the moment to remain

eventually he said, i have many questions
she answered, i know

4

two people were walking within cloisters
the chanting of monks emanated subdued
from a medieval chapel in proximity
it was the week before Palm sunday

my good teacher, the woman said
let us review the events of holy week

the man who was dressed like a monk
looked at her with great kindness

it began with the triumphal entry
people were overjoyed by his arrival
not even the stones could be kept quiet
but the world did not recognize him
his disciples did not yet comprehend
how he was to fulfill his mission

they came closer to the chapel
listening to the singing of the monks
she recognized Gregorian chants of lent

this music holds indescribable beauty
it is a call from a world of opaqueness
to one of undimmed everlasting light

the holy week is a transition
from darkness to light
from the confusion of the temporal
to the clarity of the eternal

it contains the darkest hour of
human experience, the deepest pain
and the bottomless ocean of despair
followed by the greatest light
and the promise of eternal love

they walked on and she continued

Movement 1

as the jar of perfume was broken
some disciples were concerned
but he said you always have the poor
remember her for what she has done
she has anointed me for my death

later that week reclining at the table he said
i have longed to share this meal with you
i will no longer drink of the fruit of the vine
before i drink it again in the kingdom of God

having loved those who were given to him
he now proved his love to the end

Peter said you will never wash my feet
he answered: if i do not wash your feet
you have no part with me

could she picture the room?

it was a passover meal
with bread and wine
but there was no lamb

he was the lamb, the spotless sacrifice
the reconciliation of heaven and earth
of form and instantiation, of logos and life

agnus dei qui tollis peccata mundi[3]

his love was for his disciples and the world
yet he knew this night all would desert him

when Judas went out it was night

she was shaking
she missed her warm garment
she thought she had forgotten it in her room
but then remembered she had given it away

why did Judas betray him? the teacher asked

they all abandoned him
the entire world betrayed him
only Judas thought what he did
was beyond God's forgiveness
but nothing is beyond God's
forgiveness, she answered

when Judas was gone he comforted the others
he was very moved and they were confused
Philip said show us the Father and it is enough
he replied whoever has seen me has seen the Father

Thomas said we do not know the way
he answered i am the way, the truth and the life

he emphasized again and again the way was love
if you love me you will obey what i command
if anyone loves me he will obey my teaching

if you love me you are glad
that i am going to the father
the father is greater than i am
as the father loves me so i love you

my command is this:
love each other as i have loved you

he prayed for himself, for them and the world
then he said the prince of this world is coming
but he has no hold on me

i am the true vine and you are the branches

praying to the Father he said
sanctify them by the truth, your word is truth
you have loved me before the creation of the world

then they went out and he was arrested

it was the darkest night
the night of suffering
the passion of the Lord
the betrayal of the Good
the crucifixion of the Logos

Movement 1

the high priest who had proclaimed that
it is better one person dies for the people
charged him under oath and demanded:
tell us are you the messiah!
then the high priest tore his clothes

next morning they brought him before Pilate
who asked him: are you a king?
he said: all on the side of truth listen to me
Pilate said: what is truth? *quid est veritas?*

Pilate brought him out to the people
behold the man! *ecce homo!*

when Pilate found no guilt with him
they forged a political accusation
they said: we have no king but Caesar

i do not think Pilate washed his hands
it was not a roman custom

there was extreme darkness
and in the end a terrible cry

my God, why have you forsaken me?

5

next day they woke up on an elven meadow
which formed a clearing in a small forest

he remembered the Easter vigil
which was solemn and beautiful
the fire outside, the *lumen christi*
that was carried into the dark church
the *exsultet*, the seven readings
starting with the creation of the world
the sudden return of triumphant music
standing beside her, kneeling beside her
praying beside her, wanting it not to end
just wanting it to be and never end
it was breaking of dawn when it did end

standing outside the monastery
she pointed toward a wooded area
let's go there and wait for sunrise
today we celebrate Easter sunday
she had a blanket that unfolded

now he looked at the early morning
he wondered if they were homeless?

she was awake guessing his thoughts

she said the foxes have holes
the birds have nests
but the son of man has
nowhere to rest his head

let me build a house for you, he said

you want to build a house for me?
my whole life i have dwelled in a tent
i will build a house for you, she replied

was there a movement under the trees?
an early mover? an unmoved mover?

Movement 1

there were no humans, only animals
rodents, birds, a glorious morning
a serene spot, a secluded garden

he asked, are you the gardener?
she said, *noli me tangere*, touch me not
for i have not risen to the father

do you know the fresco by Fra Angelico
in the convent of San Marco? he asked

i do know the fresco, she replied

yesterday you gave an amazing summary
an evaluation of philosophical attempts

i talked nonsense

i remember otherwise

she looked at him and said
some people say you are crazy now
they say you were great before
but now you are crazy
but i say you were crazy before not now

i remember another painting, he said
Christ rises with a banner of victory
on his right the guards are asleep, the trees are bare
on his left a guard is awakening, the trees are in bud
the world is being renewed

it is by Piero della Francesca, she said

so what happened this night?
you gave a beautiful speech
a summary, a judgment, a ruling
you also prayed on the forest floor

it was part of the *exsultet*

i have heard it often, she replied

then she looked at him and said
Christ has risen! may the never
ending joy of Easter fill your heart!

Easter is a glimpse of paradise
it's a new day, it's a new life

be who God means you to be
and you will set the world on fire

later she asked him
what do you want to do now?

he realized that for the first time
in his life he wanted nothing at all
the insight was one of sublime joy

let's find some food, she proposed

will i really get something to eat?
will i see you eat with my own eyes?
i will not believe it until i see it

you will see and believe but blessed are
those who do not see and yet believe

they found a place that offered food
the Easter sunday lunch brought them
back into realm of the material world

would you like to talk about science?
he asked, science is easy to behold

*grau teurer freund ist alle theorie
aber grün des lebens goldener baum*[4]

i am always eager to learn, she replied

the advancement of science is impressive

in this age of scientific enlightenment
scientists forget—may they be forgiven!
the dominance of what is unknowable

Movement 1

behind us is finite knowledge
before us is unchartered infinity
and this state will never change
as every age is equidistant from God

do you think so? she wondered

the universe was born 13.8 billion years ago
we use the term "big bang" for the natural
process which generates a new universe

are you implying the big bang need not
be the very act of creation? she asked

this is my intended meaning, he replied

i understand, she said, God's action is not
in competition with any scientific process
God is needed for the big bang equally
as for upholding any moment of existence

lowering his eyes he thought
her essence is His Wisdom
her instantiation is His Love

she looked at a group of children
in the distance—go on, she said

our sun lit up 4.6 billion years ago
our earth was born soon afterwards
then she was hit by another planet
this encounter gave rise to the moon

when you look up into the night sky
and gaze at the moon then remember
although tiny it is as old as one third
the age of the universe

our stage here is small but ancient
she said

the origin of life on earth could have
happened around 4 billion years ago
at first it was a world of prokaryotes
they are simple cells without organelles

after 2 billion years eukaryotes evolved
these are intricate cells with organelles
they gave rise to complex multi-cellularity
and later to animals, fungi, and plants

the last great discovery in that series
is the origin of human language itself

language is a special trait because
it generates a new mode of evolution
that goes beyond genetic reproduction

human language enables new media
for replicating information which can
be shaped by mutation and selection

evolutionary dynamics now unfold
in all aspects of human learning
including artificial intelligence

they had coffee after their meal
nearby someone read Anna Karenina
the book made his mind wander...

he did not dare to look at her directly
yet he was aware of her presence
as he was of the sun without looking

all people were divided into two sets
in one set were all people except her
in the other set was she alone

where are you now, my friend?
she said, you are easily distracted
we were talking about physics...

Movement 1

for a long time physicists thought that
the universe was static and unchanging
in their equations Newton and Einstein
felt the need to explain a fixed universe

but the great insight last century was
the universe is not static but changing
it had a beginning, it is expanding

it is aging—star formation has peaked
fewer stars will be born in the future
inevitably there will be no new stars
and the existing ones will die

galaxies are moving away from another
if the universe is expanding forever then
the distant future is cold and bleak

a universe without stars is dark
but i guess we are talking about
a very distant future, she said

only some 10^{14} years, he replied

even black holes do not live forever
the larger they are the longer they live
the largest have about 10^{100} years

nothing in the material realm is forever
she said, but what matters is that we
have enough time to find our way to God

a fundamental principle in physics widely
taken for granted is conservation of energy
energy is converted but never gained or lost

Emmy Noether showed conservation of energy
follows from time invariance of physical laws

she leaned forward and asked
does a big bang violate conversation of energy?

good question! he remarked

the big bang generates many massive particles
and mass is certainly equivalent to energy
so does a big bang generate energy?

it turns out that the likely answer is:
the gravitational field caused by the mass
balances the energy stored in the mass

generating a new gravitational field
where there was none before provides
the energy needed to build the matter
which causes that gravitational field
the two energies cancel each other out

if the total energy of the universe is zero
she remarked, the universe is a free lunch

after paying the bill for their lunch they left
they were looking for a quiet place

perhaps there are many big bangs, she said
each one giving rise to a separate universe
each universe having different properties
these universes may need time to digest
their free lunches which are substantial

if time is within those universes then
is eternity around them? she wondered

the big bang induced a sequence
of dramatic events, he continued

the first 10^{-32} seconds were
dominated by rapid expansion

as the universe increased in size
it decreased in temperature
after a microsecond protons
and neutrons started to form

after one hundredth of a second
the process of nuclear fusion began
lasting for only a few minutes
it produced hydrogen and helium

Movement 1

after three hundred thousand years
the universe was cold enough for
an event called recombination
the negatively charged electrons
recombined with positive nuclei

the universe became transparent
photons can now travel through
the universe without constantly
bumping into absorbing electrons

i'm glad the universe is transparent
she thought

the big bang allowed a few minutes of
nuclear fusion then it became too cold
but in stars nuclear fusion continued
generating many chemical elements

the first generation of stars
consisted of hydrogen and helium
because of that they were large

large stars are short lived
they become supernovas
at the end of their lives

supernovas produce further
elements in the periodic table

with those elements present
smaller stars could form
small stars are long lived

our sun which is medium sized
has a life time of 10 billion years
she has passed half of her life

smaller stars—so called red dwarfs
can live a thousand times longer
that is 10 trillion years

the vast time scales of the material
realm never fail to astonish, she said

stars are born by gravitational collapse
of molecular clouds, he continued

supernovas create pressure waves
which cause star formation in their wake

multiple stars are generated simultaneously
our sun was born together with sisters
for some time this cluster of sisters
traveled together around the galaxy
but then gravitational interactions
with other stars separated them

our galaxy, Milky Way, is spiral shaped
it has a diameter of 100000 light years

our sun is located 30000 light years
from the center of the galaxy
she takes about 225 million years
to make one orbit around that center

our solar system was also formed
by gravitational collapse of star dust

originally there were more planets
while some collided with each other
others were thrown out of our system

where are they now? she asked

drifting in the galaxy in a chilly void
without a star to keep them warm

the closest neighboring stars to us
are only a few light years away

the gravitational dominance of the sun
extends about one light year

a light year is the distance that light
travels in empty space in one year
each second light covers 300000 km

Movement 1

our moon is one light second away
the sun is 8 light minutes from us
Jupiter is 45 light minutes from the sun

the nearest known star which is called
Proxima Centauri is 4.2 light years away
it is moving toward us with a speed
of 22 kilometers per second
it reaches its closest proximity
of 3.1 light years in 27000 years
then it will depart again
the local stars influence each other
gravitational pulls bring them together
or move them apart

many planets have been discovered
which orbit other stars
there are various observational methods
one of them is that the light coming
from the star to us is slightly dimmed
when the planet is in front of the star

if this occurs in regular intervals
then we can calculate the orbital time
of that planet and even the mass

but is it not unlikely she said that
the planet orbits in a way that it is
precisely between us and its star?

yes it is unlikely but there are so many
stars that for some the orbital plane of
the planet is perfectly aligned

Proxima Centauri has a planet with a mass
that is only slightly bigger than earth
the planet is very close to the star
but since the luminosity of the star
is much less than that of our sun
the planet is in a habitable zone
where life might be possible

could we travel there? she asked

a conventional space craft as it could
be built now would take 70000 years
but then the star is moving away from us
faster than the speed of the space ship

she seemed disappointed

at a distance of 40 light years
the ultra-cool dwarf Trappist-1
boasts seven terrestrial planets
three of them in the habitable zone
our galaxy contains 100 billion stars
the current estimate is there are roughly
one billion earth-like planets around them

earth-like means to have the right mass
and be at the right distance from the star

biology wants a slim temperature range
and a rich combinatorial chemistry
large planets are loaded with hydrogen
and tend to have rather dull chemistry

the stars in our galaxy are arranged
in a thin disc and therefore most
stars are within a narrow band
on the night sky but everywhere
around us are other galaxies

those galaxies can be very far away

our neighbor the Andromeda galaxy
is at a distance of 2 million light years

Andromeda is more luminous
and more massive than our galaxy
but she has predominantly old stars
her current birth rate of stars is low

Movement 1

Andromeda will collide with Milky Way
in about 4 billion years; the resulting
fusion galaxy is called Milkomeda

how amusing! she exclaimed
to name a material object
that will exist so far in the future

the nucleus of the local supercluster
of galaxies is 60 million light years away
it can be seen in the star sign virgo
thus it is called the virgo cluster

the furthest known galaxies
are 33 billion light years away

galaxies form large filaments in the universe
between them are vast expanses of emptiness

the observable universe is a sphere
we are in the center of the sphere
its diameter is 93 billion light years
which amounts to 10^{27} meters

everything in that sphere could
in principle be observed by us
from any point within the sphere
there would have been enough time
since the big bang for light to reach us

why is the radius not 13.8 billion light years
which is the time since the big bang? she asked

this is the right question! he replied
the answer is that in addition to light
traveling the space itself is expanding

the cosmic microwave background radiation
which we can measure now was emitted
when the universe became transparent
some 380000 years after the big bang

this radiation was emitted by matter
that has now condensed into galaxies
which are estimated to be at a distance
of 46.5 billion light years from us

the observable universe is a sphere
around each observer—every location
has its own observable universe
the spheres may overlap depending
on the distance between the observers

there is a further subtlety
light that is emitted now from
a distant point in our observable
universe may never reach us
even if we allow for an infinite future
the reason is that space is expanding

if we are interested in the set
of all points that have the property
that a signal emitted there now
would eventually reach us
then we derive a smaller sphere
with a radius of 16 billion light years

there are about 10^{12} galaxies
in our observable universe

depending on the model of cosmology
the actual universe can be much larger

the galaxies within the observable universe
may only be a small fraction of all galaxies

the story has a few more surprises

the total amount of ordinary matter
in the observable universe is 10^{51} kg
which comes to 10^{80} protons or neutrons

Movement 1

but the energy content of the universe
is given by the following accounting:
5% ordinary matter, 27% dark matter
68% dark energy

dark matter and dark energy are postulated
phenomena to explain certain observations

dark matter is a conjectured form of matter
that has gravitational interaction with ordinary
matter but no electromagnetic interaction

the primary evidence for dark matter is
that many galaxies would disintegrate
by centrifugal forces if they did not contain
additional matter which is unseen—dark

the nature of dark energy is more elusive
the main evidence is the observation that
the expansion of the universe is speeding up

dark energy exerts an unknown force
which pushes galaxies away from each other
dark energy is thought to fill space uniformly
it is not even diluted when space expands

you need good imagination for this, she said
are physicists out of resources here?

aided by mathematics the high priests of physics
are never out of resource, he replied

she was silent

he assumed—incorrectly—that her interest
in astronomy had ceased for the time being

they continued their Easter walk
marveling at the various joys of life
they saw people in conversation
children at play running over fields
with yellow and white flowers

she thought that all people consisted
of baryons made in the big bang
they were of that primordial dust
which was later refined in stars
and eventually here on earth
put in touch with the breath of life

she thought of light so fast and so slow
that it was suspended forever traversing
the vast voids of expanding space time

why is the universe so large?
what message is revealed herein?

the answer could lie within physics
a smaller universe may be unstable

the answer could lie within biology
a smaller universe could be unable
to bring about origins of life

the answer could lie in mathematics
a smaller universe could be unable
to manifest the infinity which is
the essence of underlying reality

but is eternity not in the moment?
infinity not in every grain of sand?

he thought of Faust and Wagner
walking on Easter sunday
outside the gates of the city
but he was not the Doctor
and she was not Margarete
neither was she Helen of Troy
nor Anna Karenina, nor Kitty
nor Dorothea of Middlemarch

as far as he could discern
she was not depicted by any
female figure in literature
known to him at the time

Movement 1

sinking into memories he whispered
Sie hören nicht die folgenden Gesänge
Die Seelen denen ich die ersten sang[5]

she replied without hesitation
i am here to hear all your songs
your first and your last

did she really say this?

later they were sitting on a bench
with cheerful crowds passing by

there are four fundamental forces
of nature, he continued in physics

gravity dominates on large scales
giving rise to galaxies, stars, planets

the electromagnetic force holds
chemical bonds between atoms
and generates visible phenomena
including the colors of nature
the leaves and the flowers
it is the force of smell and touch
of reproduction and of death

the electromagnetic force
enables us to sit on this bench
without falling through it
pulled down by gravity

then there are the two forces
that act in the atomic nucleus
they are called strong and weak

the weak force is involved
in radioactive decay of atoms
the weak force mysteriously
violates mirror symmetry

it was long held as a law of nature
that a universe and its mirror image
would behave in the same way but
the weak force falls out of line here

finally there is the strong force
which confines quarks into hadrons
such as neutrons and protons
each of them contains three quarks

the energy of the strong force field
generates the mass of hadrons while
the quarks contribute only 1 percent

the mass that resides in material objects
comes from the energy of the strong force

the strong force also binds protons
and neutrons together in atomic nuclei

the nucleus of the hydrogen atom
contains a single proton
other atoms have several protons
and neutrons in their nucleus

the number of protons defines the
chemical element, one for hydrogen
two for helium, and so on
six for carbon, eight for oxygen

at the length scale of 10^{-15} meters
which is the diameter of a proton
the strong force is 137 times stronger
than the electromagnetic force
10^6 times stronger than the weak force
and 10^{38} times stronger than gravity

are these four the only forces? she asked

one does not know for sure, he replied
many phenomena have been described
but many questions are unanswered

the theory of the strong force is called
quantum chromodynamics because
quarks have "color"

i thought color is electromagnetic, she said

it is another kind of color, he replied

the standard model of particle physics is a
theory describing three of the four forces
electromagnetic, weak, and strong

the standard model enjoys great success
in making numerous experimental predictions
but it leaves certain phenomena unexplained
maybe because it does not contain gravity

the standard model does not describe
dark matter nor dark energy...

for the first time today he sensed
that the afternoon was progressing
he was aware that sooner rather
than later they would have to part

let me find a bearing, she said
first we traversed the macrocosm
then we dissected the microcosm
now you want to fit them together

physicists want to know all, he said
they are not to blame!

Faust exclaimed, *zwar weiß ich viel
doch möcht ich alles wissen!*
Mephisto countered, *vieles ist mir
bewußt doch allwissend bin ich nicht*[6]

the standard model is a theory
which brings three forces into one system
but there is no approach yet
which succeeds in incorporating gravity

string theory attempts to do this
string theory is a collective name
for a number of possible theories
but no one knows which of them
really applies to our universe

a unified theory of all of physics
has remained elusive so far

they were silent now

he wished the joy of Easter
to remain forever and ever

6

in the evening she came home
she opened the door to her room
which was always unlocked

then she switched on a light
from a drawer she took a photo
and placed it on the bed

she knelt down
on the wall before her was the cross
she had received at her first communion

she looked at the image
with sadness and tender love

then with a single finger
without touching the surface
she traced the eyebrows
of the face on the photo

she whispered... happy Easter!
i am the resurrection and the life
...you are in me and i am in you

she moved between prayer and
conversation recalling memories
which were both happy and sad
in the end she prayed quietly

eventually she took the photo
and put it back into the drawer

she walked to the table
on it were some books
pencils and sheets of paper
a card showing Holman Hunt's
Light of the World

she found a small Easter bunny
inspected it and smiled

she took a small bag, a towel
and walked out of the room
leaving the door ajar

when she came back
she was changed for the night
she put her day clothes over
the chair, turned off the lamp

she sat down on the bed
her face toward the door
she adopted the lotus position
she sat motionless for an hour
then she laid down and fell asleep

her sleep was blessed by the gods
interspersed with vivid dreams
of quarks, hadrons, and galaxies
of small and of large worlds

in one dream she found herself
in a shepherd's hut huddled in hay
a poet stood before her in moonlight
holding a weaved cap in his hands

in another dream was a fountain
and a king kneeling before her
offering her a book with both hands

she analyzed the conversations
of today, yesterday and tomorrow

regarding that one crucial question
she came down on the side of...
self-evident in itself... and to her

7

by now it was early summer
they cycled to the river

in the adjacent riparian forests
were wide bodies of water
that were already warm
and beautiful for swimming

she took off her outer clothes
wearing a swimsuit underneath
she walked toward the water
probed it with her toes and dove in

they were floating under trees
that were raining seeds on them

when i was a child, she said
i thought the trees made the wind
and the mountains carried the sky

i grew up near mountains
there was a pristine lake
in which i loved to swim
it was fed from cold streams

in the summer when it was hot
we jumped into the icy brooks
their waters came from the blue
glaciers that were high above

but in a warm pond like this
we could move from inanimate
matter to life—do you agree?

what is life? how did it start?
where do we come from?

all creatures on earth are related
and trace back in their ancestry
to the same origin of life, he said
we are sprung from one source

earth formed soon after the sun
young earth was hot because of
gravitational collapse and impacts

over time she cooled down steadily
at some point she was calm enough
for water to collect on the surface
this was around 4 billion years ago

as early as then there could have been
an origin of life, maybe in a warm pond

like this one here? she asked diving
could there be origins of new life
here now? she asked re-emerging

unlikely, he said, life once present is greedy
and gulps down all available food sources
this leaves little room for new origins

to imagine a scenario for the beginning
consider the components of living matter

the main building blocks of life are
DNA, RNA, proteins, lipids, sugars

in cells genetic information is stored as DNA
information flows from DNA to RNA to proteins
DNA specifies which RNAs are produced
RNAs specify which proteins are built

DNA is the aperiodic crystal which
Schrödinger imagined in "What is life?"

RNA stores information and catalyzes reactions
proteins catalyze reactions and provide structure

Movement 1

RNA and DNA are long molecules
consisting of strings of nucleotides
they are sequences over an alphabet

for DNA the alphabet is A, T, C, G
for RNA the alphabet is A, U, C, G
A stands for adenine, T for thymine
C for cytosine, G for guanine, U for uracil

in DNA the nucleotides form base pairs
DNA is passed from parent to offspring
from the dividing cell to its daughters

as they were floating side by side
they observed a line of ducklings
mannerly following their mother

life on earth is cell-based, he said
membranes of cells consist of lipids

the chemicals of life are natural substances
which can arise under certain conditions
amino acids which make up proteins
are found in meteorites that fall on earth

lipids can self-assemble into vesicles
which can serve as precursors of cells
they can divide spontaneously

for an origin of life we also need
all the building blocks of RNA
and they have to form polymers

once we have strings of RNA
they can catalyze further processes

strings of RNA can make copies
of themselves by base pairing

RNA could populate proto-cells
and help them to divide better

the willow trees on the bank were
standing close with some of their
hanging branches touching the water

if all is chemistry then what is life?
when does life appear? she asked

"prelife" is a theory that explains
how chemistry becomes biology
prelife is a mix of chemicals that has
the ability to assemble information
prelife has selection and mutation
but lacks direct reproduction

the transition from prelife to life
is marked by the onset of reproduction

prior to the theory of prelife
reproduction was seen as prerequisite
for mutation and natural selection
but prelife reverses that order
in prelife reproduction arises
by mutation and selection

she swam effortlessly which made him think
that she was highly adapted to the aquatic
environment of her evolutionary ancestors

chemical reactions are described by mathematics
the resulting formalism specifies chemical kinetics
a similar formalism can be used for evolution

the attempt for delineation is:
chemistry has no reproduction
biology has reproduction

tell me more about prelife, she said

prelife is a chemistry of polymers
these are sequences of nucleotides

Movement 1

the sequences form at different rates
some of them gain higher prevalence
the resulting selection is relevant
because it can guide an origin of life

the chemical reactions of prelife are subject
to thermal noise which results in mutation

therefore prelife is mutation and selection
but without reproduction

prelife solves a relevant problem: it generates
a continuous transition from non-life to life
there is no need for one magical giant leap

unnoticeably chemistry becomes richer
at some point chemistry turns into biology

once biology is there it asks many questions
where do i come from? where will i go? she said

presumably prelife generated many origins of life
which competed until a single one prevailed

could two origins of life fuse to become
one life eventually? she wondered

i like that idea! they were now looking
in a low angle over the water surface

there is a river to the east of here
which flowers in the spring, she said
insects emerge from it to live for one day
during which they make love and die

the phenomenon reminds me of life itself
which emerges from the river of time
flourishes for a brief day in the universe
and then goes out again without a trace

he was silent

are we sure that an origin of our life
occurred on this planet? she asked

we are not sure but all think it is a likely scenario
alternatively earth could have been fertilized
by bacterial spores coming from another planet
that formed long before our own solar system

life could have originated on that planet
rocks of this planet with bacterial spores
could have been in the molecular cloud
which gave rise to our solar system
such rocks could have fallen onto earth
where the spores found good conditions

but this process is thought to be unlikely
because the spores would have to survive
very adverse conditions before reaching us

we could as well entertain the possibility
that intelligent beings visited young earth
and seeded her with bacterial spores
thus conducting a planetary experiment

what we know is that 3.5 billion years ago
prokaryotes were abundant on earth
they comprise archaea and bacteria

on the top of biological classification
archaea, bacteria, and eukaryotes
constitute the three domains of life

domains of life! how grand! she said
how did those microbes make their living?

cells reproduce by division which
means one cell splits into two cells
for this to happen cells must rebuild
their molecular components, he said

Movement 1

since life is based on carbon chemistry
cells need to build carbon compounds
carbon was present in the atmosphere
of our young planet in the form of CO_2

life discovered photosynthesis
which is a chemical reaction that
turns CO_2 into carbohydrates

the energy for this reaction is provided
by sunlight but other chemical compounds
are needed for the exchange of electrons

a potential electron donor is ferric iron
which was abundant in the early oceans

as life prospered cells started battling
over limiting resources: a hotly contested
nutrient was phosphate which is needed
for DNA, RNA, and other molecules

often competing cells would use all phosphate
in a place and then cell division stalled

but sometimes ferric iron was more limiting
then cell division could not proceed although
the precious phosphate was still present

life needed a revolutionary new idea
to make good use of such situations
could one overcome the dependency
on ferric iron as electron donor?

the task was solved by cyanobacteria
instead of iron they accessed a more
abundant source of electrons: water!

but to access the electrons in water
you must split a very stable molecule
cyanobacteria found a chemical reaction
which was powerful enough to do this
this reaction was a game changer!

oxygenic photosynthesis, she announced

indeed! its discovery was a unique event
in the history of life on our planet
it was never discovered a second time
all plants and all other organisms
that perform oxygenic photosynthesis
utilize the tools found by cyanobacteria

essentially all life on earth ultimately depends
on the fixation of carbon from the atmosphere
organisms that do this are primary producers
predators cannot exist without them

are we predators? she asked

much worse! he replied

we are destroyers of entire ecosystems
something has gone wrong in our evolution
we need to fix that—but we are getting ahead
let us stay in the distant past for now

oxygenic photosynthesis started 3 billion years ago
originally the cyanobacteria remained a minority
they were marginalized by other microbes which
used iron for non-oxygenic photosynthesis

cyanobacteria only dominated in places where
ferric iron was scarce and phosphate was abundant
they were sidelined, but their waste product
—oxygen—was about to upset the world order

there was almost no free oxygen in the atmosphere
of young earth but by about 2.4 billion years ago
there was a sudden increase in oxygen

over a period of tens of millions of years
the oxygen concentration rose 1000 fold
this cataclysmic moment is called
the great oxygenation event or GOE

why did the GOE happen at that time?

Movement 1

this is the right question because
cyanobacteria evolved hundreds of
millions of years prior to the GOE

over a long time there was continuous
production of oxygen by cyanobacteria
and removal by geochemical processes
this situation led to a steady state
with low oxygen levels in the atmosphere

then what happened at the GOE? she asked

the timing of the GOE was set by the planet
the GOE coincided with a major event in geology:
the formation of the first continents
before then there were islands and archipelagos

as continents formed less ferric iron was released
but more phosphor withered from rocks
both changes favored cyanobacteria

as they became more abundant they released
more oxygen which rusted the ferric iron
further undercutting their competitors

the increase in oxygen led to a feedback loop
it shifted the balance to a new equilibrium
which was dominated by cyanobacteria

now for the first time large quantities
of free oxygen were in the atmosphere

the path was laid for further events
the world was on the eve of the eukaryotic expansion

for two billion years prokaryotes had enjoyed
an exclusive reign but this was about to change

somewhere on the globe, somewhere in the ocean
one bacterium swallowed another with consequences

this was atypical because bacteria do not swallow
each other—if it occurs then nothing happens
maybe the engulfed bacterium gets digested
or the greedy gulper dies from congestion

but this one time both lived and
they gave rise to a lineage of offspring

the two bacteria—one inside the other—
over time evolved to help one another
this process is called endosymbiosis

the internal bacterium became
the mother of all mitochondria
the true mitochondrial Eve

the complex of the two became the ancestor
of all eukaryotes, of all higher cells
of all plants, fungi, animals, you, and me

mitochondria are organelles inside higher cells
they are responsible for providing energy
they are the power stations of the cell
they burn sugar and produce molecules
which can release energy when needed

fundamentally the origin of eukaryotes
is associated with an aerobic life cycle
mitochondria perform respiration
they inhale oxygen and burn sugar
they exhale CO_2 and provide energy

why did this lifestyle arise at that time?

because then there was enough free oxygen
in the atmosphere and in the vast oceans

endosymbiosis led to the first eukaryotic cell
later there were other instances of endosymbiosis
but they involved a eukaryotic cell swallowing
eukaryotes like to swallow other cells
that's what they do

in our unfolding story we have covered
two unique events in the history of life
first the discovery of oxygenic photosynthesis
second the emergence of the eukaryotic cell

eukaryotes also became primary producers
and evolved to use oxygenic photosynthesis
the organelle in eukaryotic cells responsible
for photosynthesis is called the chloroplast
it came from endosymbiosis of a cyanobacterium
all pieces of the puzzle fit together!

after the GOE the oxygen concentration in the
atmosphere was constant for 1.6 billion years
but then approximately 800 million years ago
the oxygen concentration started to rise again

this time oxygen was produced jointly
by photosynthetic prokaryotes and eukaryotes

in the Neoproterozoic Oxygenation Event (NOE)
the oxygen level rose 10-100 fold within a few hundred
million years; it was a second but smaller step

again it is likely that earth herself made the call
because the time coincides with the breakup of
the supercontinent into smaller continents

this event can be associated with a decreased rate
at which oxygen is removed from the atmosphere

about 600 million years ago the oxygen
concentration reached its current value

then we have initial radiation of complex animals
for the first time macroscopic organisms emerge

the reason for the timing is compelling:
an obstacle for large aerobic organisms
is how to bring oxygen into the interior
the solution of the problem becomes easier
if there is high oxygen concentration

diverse animal body plans emerged
during the early Cambrian period
which began 541 million years ago

plants were the first to move
from the oceans onto the land
they were followed by arthropods

scorpions were the first land animals
tetrapod vertebrates make a landfall
some 380 million years ago

we have almost reached the present...

shall we make a landfall here? she suggested

they found a warm sandy spot on the bank
of the great river zooming by

noises of people were at a distance
sometimes boats passed in the river
slowly upstream or quickly downstream
the river was flowing in time and space

Vishnu glides on the river of time, she said
usually he is asleep attended by his faithful
consort Lakshmi—what a bliss!
occasionally he wakes up to save a world

are you now asleep or awake? he asked

i am awake, i am so awake, she laughed
ready to go and to save a world or two!

may i recapitulate for us? she wondered
glancing at him sideways

please do, he answered

there are four eons of earth history
in the beginning was the Hadean
named after Hades brother of Zeus
and king of the underworld

Movement 1

the name emphasizes hellish conditions
with high temperatures caused by gravitational
collapse, radioactivity, and frequent collisions
with other bodies of the solar system

the period lasted from the formation
of earth until 4 billion years ago

due to high atmospheric pressure
liquid water could have been present
in some places on the surface

he looked at her while she continued
watching the river zooming by

next came the Archean named after
the greek word for "beginning"
it was the beginning of the geological age
and lasted from 4 to 2.5 billion years

the oldest rock formations found
on earth are from the Archean
they occur in Greenland, Canada,
Montana, Wyoming, Scotland,
the Baltic Shield, India, Brazil,
Western Australia, South Africa

in contrast the zircon minerals
of the Hadean are mere grains

all riches of the world are mere grains
of sand when compared to her, he thought

whether the origin of life occurred
in the Hadean or Archean is unknown
certain is that during the second half
of the Archean the planet was alive

space travelers from afar would
have found a planet of bacteria
and an atmosphere without oxygen

would they have known to come back
a few billion years in the future to check
for further developments? she wondered

toward the end of the Archean
the crust had cooled down enough
to allow the formation of continents

the Archean witnessed oxygenic photosynthesis
and the beginning of accumulation of oxygen
but the GOE itself brings us to the next eon

she stopped to watch two buoyant people drifting
downstream in an old fashioned rowing boat
she thought that those people and their boat
were consequences of biological events long ago

why were they here? where were they headed?
she did not know that the joyful passersby were
Dr Negria and the infamous Editha Pastree
who belonged to the depth of other years
by a clerical error they appeared here
such mutations are bound to happen
in large libraries of books and genomes

she continued after some time

the third eon, the Proterozoic, spans the time
from 2.5 billion to 541 million years ago
the name means "earlier life"

at the beginning of the Proterozoic
was the GOE at the end the NOE
during the Proterozoic oxygen levels rose
from nearly nothing to current values

the earth was tectonically very active
supercontinents formed and broke into pieces
mountains arose, the first glaciation occurred
there is even evidence for a snowball earth

Movement 1

the Proterozoic saw the endosymbiotic events
which lead to higher cells
the exclusive reign of prokaryotes ended
soft-bodied multi-cellular life forms appeared

the first three eons together constitute
the Precambrian supereon

she was now resolved to go all the way
holding back nothing she wanted it all

the fourth eon, the Phanerozoic
begins with the Cambrian period
Phanerozoic means "visible life"
the eon lasts until here and now
it is the current period of earth history

during this time tectonic forces caused
the continents to move and collect into
a single landmass known as Pangaea
which split into the current continents

the eon began with the evolution
of animals and plants which spread
from the oceans to colonize the land

the eon witnessed five mass extinctions
caused by various catastrophic events
such as sudden increase in volcanic activity
or a large comet hitting earth

mass extinctions mark the end of one
world order and the beginning of a new one
the ages of reptiles, dinosaurs, mammals

humans are now causing the sixth great
mass extinction... and we have to stop this
from happening! do you agree?

have i said all of this? he wondered

8

they were at a staircase near the center of the city
a book had been written about this place he loved

it was a Saturday afternoon in the midst of summer
the city had gone out into the surrounding nature
to celebrate this day and thus the stairs lay deserted

also on a Saturday afternoon but many years earlier
someone of that novel had walked down the stairs
to visit a woman who waited for him wearing rainbow
colors in an otherwise pristine white apartment

mi adorada querida[7]—he thought of Buenos Aires

she looked at him

memories are loops in space time which return
like recurrent states in stochastic universes

we have discussed the unfolding of life
some aspects of evolutionary biology
have the flavor of historical studies
we need to find out what happened
for what reason and at what time
we explore environmental conditions
that lead to one change or another
but the main question is: what drives
the process that moves living matter
from simple origins toward complexity?
is evolution ascending stairs?

they sat down on top of the stairs

evolution is the process
that organizes living matter
its mathematical description
is called evolutionary dynamics

but what is it that evolves?

often we talk about evolution of cells,
genes, genomes, organisms, species
but the carrier of the evolutionary process
is the population—only populations evolve!

populations consist of individuals
individuals can be of different types
the types are heritable to an extent
they have persistence in spacetime

dissecting the process of evolution
we encounter mutation and selection

mutation means new types emerge over time
selection means types grow at different rates
mutation and selection are two fundamental
forces of the evolutionary process

they are not forces as in physics
but they move the mix of a population
they move the abundance of types
relative abundance is called frequency
frequencies change over time
—this is evolution

is all that we find in the living world
a sequel of mutation and selection?
she wondered

these are the two fundamental aspects
upon which we can elaborate, he replied

evolution is a mathematical process
everything that we talk about here
has a mathematical representation

evolution started as a verbal theory
but the mathematical formulation
followed and became indispensable

many verbal debates in evolution
resolve in the light of mathematics
mathematics is available light
it does not leave us out of resource

they observed two people ascending
the stairs: possibly a father and a son

if different types of individuals
have the same reproductive rate
we are left with random drift
which leads to neutral evolution

even here by chance some types
become more abundant than others

if we wait long enough one type wins
then all individuals in the population
are the descendants of one individual
which is the common ancestor
of all present and future individuals
—assuming asexual reproduction

asexual reproduction means
each individual has one parent
sexual reproduction means that
individuals have two or more parents

more than two? she asks

anything goes in biology, he replied

many animals are sex obsessed and incestuous
they reproduce only sexually and then
they always mate with similar partners

in the wider realm of microbes however
cells reproduce asexually normally
and sexually only sometimes as needed
but if sexually they are willing to try
partners that are extremely different
they can incorporate genetic material
from very distant bacterial species
they can try out any available DNA
thus a cell could end up with genetic
material from multiple other cells

Movement 1

they tend to use sexual reproduction
if the environment becomes adverse
if their prospects are turning dim
they are willing to roll the dice of sex

sexual reproduction is a gamble
sexual reproduction shuffles genomes
and produces hopeful new variants

asexual reproduction is a game
that generates more of the same
more of what is already proven

asexual reproduction is still
subject to point mutations
and insertions and deletions
but it does not mix two genomes
it does not use recombination

let us paint a picture of evolution
a somewhat simplified representation
a colorful picture with... rainbows
our picture will not stay in the plane
it will move upward to many dimensions...

he paused

in the book the white room
moved upward like a gondola
when the rainbow colors
were spread on the floor

Gemahne mich nicht des Gewesenen[8]
—who spoke like this?

from the window of the white room
you could see the hills in the distance

what is on your mind? she wondered
is it a visit from another time?

with great tenderness she turned to him
i sense you long to tell me another story
do you have memories of those stairs
that are leading up to us in the present?

her eyes were warm and inviting

can she read my thoughts?

there are some books, he said
that become our own memories
we recall events in those books
as if they were part of our life

the book of our life fuses with others
resulting in a recombination of books
as if there was a sexual reproduction
of books, of lives, of living trajectories

they looked over the staircase

know that Sigmund (not Freud but Karl)
as a teenager walking up those stairs
with his father met Schrödinger (Erwin)
descending the stairs—*What is Life?*

a few steps from here Mendel was a student
Gödel proved his incompleteness theorem
Mach and Boltzmann clashed over atoms
the staircase is an *art nouveau* masterpiece

over there was the house of the blue unicorn
where the protagonist as high school student
met a beautiful young woman with red hair

she was the good spirit of this district
and over unicorns they became friends

some say unicorns exist in potentiality
but not in actuality—i find their purported
non-existence in actuality irrelevant

there was an academy which offered
education for a career in diplomacy
someone played the piano beautifully

Movement 1

one day it was the Schubert f-minor sonata
the high school student delivered a message
and asked him about the science of grammar
this was before Chomsky, he added

the street was called differently then
but it is now named after Boltzmann

because atoms do exist, she said

and unicorns don't, he replied

near the bottom of the stairs
was the apartment of another
who was simply taken along

before the war he hunted a bear in Bosnia
whose fur was spread out in his room
carefully preserved—i can recall the smell

beyond the square bustling with traffic
beyond the railway was the white apartment
from which you saw the hills in the distance

did the lady with the red hair live there?

she had a small house with a garden
and a beautiful daughter eventually
someone else lived in that apartment

who are you in that book? she asked

i am nobody, i am not in that book
i am not in any book, i am not an actor
only a lost observer, a lonely dreamer

you are my dream, he thought
then i am your life, she thought

are there any events in your memory
for which you were an actor? she asked

various people met at the staircase
he said, they walked over the stairs
and they admired them

nearby was a restaurant and a cafe
on the other side of the bridge
was a park where they played tennis

the book laments a time which is no more
even back then it was already gone

like the poem half way down by the fountain
shall we go there and read it? he suggested

she held him back, wait...

look into my eyes, she said
he tried to do so but trembled

please look into my eyes

Wenn die Blätter..., she began

keep looking!

Wenn die Blätter auf den Stufen liegen
herbstlich atmet aus den alten Stiegen
was vor Zeiten über sie gegangen
Mond darin sich zweie dicht umfangen hielten
leichte Schuh und schwere Tritte
die bemooste Vase in der Mitte
überdauert Jahre zwischen Kriegen

Viel ist hingesunken uns zur Trauer
und das Schönste zeigt die kleinste Dauer[9]

there was silence

he said, you do know the poem?
i assumed you would not know it
...or do you know the book too?

it was extremely quiet around them
she did not answer his question

after some time he exhaled, who are you?

a few moments later barely audible, he said
i do not ask why you know the poem
i simply ask: who are you?

MOVEMENT 2

1

good teacher, where have i come from?
and why your efforts at teaching me?

you came here long ago
you were completely alone
you stood in front of the gate
you did not strike the bell
you did not draw attention
you just waited patiently
until someone noticed you

when a woman passed by
you showed her the letter
it was a folded piece of paper
with a few words written on it
the woman could not read them
but she asked you to come inside

various people looked at the letter
and eventually it was deciphered
"with this child i am sending you
an image of the goddess of wisdom"

no such image was found on you
and everyone was surprised
but they decided to let you stay
and find a home in the village

you were admitted to school
and then as the years passed
the teachers began to realize
the true meaning of the letter

you yourself were the image
you excelled in every subject
brightly you shone in wisdom
and in all matters of the heart

eventually the teachers decided
that they had presented to you
all they knew themselves

they searched for other teachers
who could take you further
they thought you were special
perhaps destined for greatness

i was one teacher they brought
i was blessed in that i was allowed
to stay here with you ever since

as for your place of origin
it was never discovered
many messengers were sent
to all villages and towns
in the vicinity and even
to some distant places

after those efforts had ceased
with no answers forthcoming
you were simply considered
a child of unknown parents

you spoke rarely in the beginning
but as soon as words flowed
you used the local dialect
you sounded as others around you

they said you ate little
whenever you could spare food
you gladly gave it to others

already as child you fed the hungry
although you were hungry yourself

they said you lived on water alone
there was something very special
about your fondness for pure water

Movement 2

you loved to swim in the lake
and in the brooks that nourished it
do you have memories of the time?

my first memories of this place
are as if coming from a dream
i am standing in front of a door
but it is none of the doors
that i am seeing here now

the door was very peculiar
it had no handle on the outside
it could only be opened from within
it was entirely overgrown
it had never been opened before

i was waiting in the morning twilight
eventually the door was opened
i was invited to come in and eat
the people were good to me

they gave me food of a kind
that i had not tasted before
they put me in a warm bed
falling asleep i prayed for them

who has taught you to pray?

God has taught me to pray
she answered quickly

God was inside the dwelling of my body
before i was—He has never left me

how did you pray that first night?

i asked God to protect those people
who were still unknown to me
to help them and give them health
happiness and meaning in their lives
then i prayed for all people

but who knows if my memory
of that first night is genuine
or if those prayers came later?
in any case my prayers are
very simple and unremarkable

do you have recollections from
the time before you came here?

i have images in my mind
but i do not know if they are
memories of events or dreams
my life is a dream...

sometimes i see a vast library
and a blind librarian

after some time she said, good teacher
why am i worthwhile to be your student?

light of my life, i return the question
why am i worthwhile to be your teacher?
or better, let me ask the converse:
why am i worthwhile to be your student?
for i am not sure who is the learner

a good teacher learns from the ignorance
of his students, she said with a smile

he said, shall we resume our lesson?
have you read the book i gave you?

i have read it, she answered
the contents are to my liking
they resonate with all that
i consider true and beautiful

would you be so kind to formulate
some of them in your own words
i long to hear the teaching from you
and experience it in a new light

she collected her thoughts and began

Movement 2

good teacher, she said, it is written
the impermanent has no reality
instead reality lies in the eternal

while the body is mortal
what dwells in the body is immortal

there was never a time when we did not exist
nor will there be a time when we cease to exist

you and i will walk side by side forever
she looked at him with penetrating eyes

the self does not die when the body dies
it cannot be pierced by weapons
it cannot be burned by fire
it rests indestructibly within us
it is everlasting and limitless
erected on the edifice of eternity

the self is eternal and cannot be harmed
the self is the knower while everything
else is the field that needs to be known

the book asks the question: how to lead life?
it compares an active with a meditative one

the book suggests the active life is preferred
do not stay with inaction but strive for action
but do not engage in action for the sake of reward
instead act without selfish attachment

if you are only motivated by the fruits of action
you become miserable, anxious, and confused

wisdom is renunciation of selfish desire
wisdom is repudiation of sense craving

yoga is not mere physical posture
but mental attitude, mental pose
yoga is perfect evenness of mind

a downward path begins with attachment
false longings breed desire for possession
desire burns to anger which clouds judgment
we cannot choose between wise and unwise

we find peace and wisdom only
if we act free from attachment

those are free who renounce selfish desire
who move beyond the veil of selfishness

life and the call for selfless action co-evolved
all life comes from God, all life leads to God

selfless acts originate in God
and bring us back to God

in all our actions we must have
the well-being of others in mind

the confused work for their own profit
the wise for the welfare of the world
the wise perform only those deeds
which are guided by compassion

the book describes human nature:
the senses are above the body
the mind is above the senses
the will is above the mind
the true self is above the will

the will is the only friend of the self
the will is the only enemy of the self

they had reached a still lake
whose surface was a mirror of the world
a swan slowly glided over the pond
without causing ripples in the water

the scene evoked in the onlookers
a sense of spiritual transcendence

there was a swan, the teacher said
who if offered a mixture of milk and water...

Movement 2

... could drink the milk alone, she completed

he was silent — then he asked her
do your memories surprise you?

do yours not surprise you? she replied

their path meandered around the lake
she continued her summary of the Gita

i love the many revelations of the Lord
who is God transcendent and immanent

*my true being is unborn and changeless
i am the Lord who dwells in every creature
i protect the good, i am present to those
who see all life as my manifestation*

*if you respond to joys and sorrows of others
as your own then you have union with me*

*i am the brilliance of the sun and the moon
i am the fragrance of earth, the radiance of fire
i am the desire that is in harmony with life*

*i am the sacred word Om
i am the taste of pure water
i am the life in every creature*

*i know everything about the past, present
and future but no one knows me entirely*

*i am attained by those who remember me
who are attached to me and nothing else*

*by undivided love you can know
the Lord who pervades all existence
who is the true self of all creatures*

*great souls seek my divine nature
they worship me with a one-pointed
mind having realized that i am the
eternal source of everything*

*i am the goal of life, the support of all
the only refuge, the one true friend*

*i am beginning, middle, and end
i am immortality and i am death
i am what is and what is not
i transcend all dualities*

*i love all creatures equally
but those who love me live in me
and i come to live in them*

*in this fleeting world give your love to me
if you seek me you will be united with me*

*those enter into me
who make me the goal of all their work
who act without selfish attachment
who devote themselves to me completely
who are free from ill will for any creature*

*they see truly who see the Lord in every creature
who see the deathless in the hearts of all that die*

*seeing the same Lord everywhere
they do not harm themselves nor others
thus they attain the supreme goal*

she was silent

around them were the sounds of nature
trees spreading cones on the forest floor
rodents and birds collecting their food

she looked through the surface
of the lake noticing the shadows
of fish projecting in various sizes

then the teacher said to her
you speak as one who understands
you do not only recite knowledge
but you transmit wisdom
your life gives meaning to the words

Movement 2

my good teacher, she said
i am only a grain of sand
i know that i know nothing

he continued
beloved light be fearless and pure
never waver in your determination
in your dedication to love give freely
be self-controlled, sincere, truthful

take joy in renunciation
learn to be detached, never be angry
never harm a living creature
be compassionate and gentle
avoid malice and pride
show good will to all people

they proceeded along the path
through the forest of tall trees
with views of the serene lake

after some time the teacher said
there was an event in your childhood
of which i have gained knowledge
it happened before i came here

he did not look at her now
therefore he did not see that
her eyes began to fill with tears

there was another child
another orphan in the village
to whom you were close
she became seriously ill
doctors were called
but could not help her

they could not separate you
you stayed with her to the end

i remember, she exclaimed
i will always remember her

she produced a small likeness
it was worn and partly faded

she said with breaking voice
hers was the greatest soul
untainted by any malice

i witnessed her suffering
she was desperate in the end
she died holding my hands
i have never recovered

he returned the image to her

after a long silence he said
what have you read in the book?

the wise do not mourn the dead
but i do, she added bursting into tears

2

they had found a courtyard
near the center of the city
there was a bench under a tree
a small lawn and some flowers
open windows were looking on

these places in town are special
they want to be discovered
they are sometimes here
and at other times elsewhere
they never stay in one location

she remembered the image
of an indian goddess
which had captivated her
when she was a child

at times the image was
in one book then in another
within a book the image moved
between pages and sometimes
it was absent all together

the goddess was alive
she could choose to make
an appearance or vanish

years later when she had grown older
the image was always in the same book
on a page whose number she knew

shall we resume our journey? she asked

living matter is compositional, he said
genes can be in one cell then another
they can swap places and invert

slowly, she said, begin at the foundation

the genome of an organism is given
by a sequence of a four letter alphabet
a small bacterial genome has a length
of about one million such letters

let us arrange all those sequences
in a grid with neighboring sequences
differing exactly by a single letter

this grid has one million dimensions
each dimension has 4 choices which
are the 4 letters of the alphabet

we are in a high dimensional space
which is discrete but not continuous

the number of points in our space
is 4 raised to one million or 10^{600000}
this is indeed a very large number
the 10^{80} hadrons in our observable
universe pale in comparison

he loved those numbers and scales
they gave him exponential delight
man is a counting ape, he thought

the combinatorial complexity of small
bacterial genomes trivializes anything
that this universe could ever instantiate

evolution of life on our planet only sees
a tiny fraction of genomic sequences

evolution unfolding on all suitable planets
of the observable universe could only search
a small part of the space spanned by genomes

life is a frivolous fragment of the possible

your genome space reminds me
of the library of Babel, she said

Borges's library of Babel? he asked

Movement 2

i often thought the realization of
that library containing all books
that are combinatorically possible
would collapse into a black hole

i remember Borges proposed
that each book had 410 pages
each page had 40 lines
each line had 80 characters
he used an alphabet of size 25
including punctuation marks

it is quite a magical place, she said
every book that was ever written
can certainly be found in the library
but every book that will be written
is also there already

every combinatorial possibility is present
no book is missing unless somebody
borrowed it and then forgot to return it
even that would not make a difference

if a plot does not fit within 410 pages
we can spread it over multiple volumes

the books which describe your past life
are there and those that predict your future

for each decision we need to take
there is a book that discusses all
arguments one way or another

there are also books questioning
everything we take for granted

alas most books in the library
mean nothing at all

whenever we hold a book in our hands
that offers one meaningful statement
we could consider it a miracle

each book is an integer
some are prime numbers
we can calculate how many
books are prime numbers

since Borges's library is finite
there is a book representing
the largest prime among them
adventurous mathematicians
might go out and search for it

of course the vast library contains
only a small fraction of integers
every finite number however large
is nothing at all compared to infinity

the total number of books in his library
is 25 raised to the power of 40 x 80 x 410
that is 25 to the power of 1.3 million
that is about 10 to the 1.8 million

let us compare the library of Babel
to the space of bacterial genomes
our bacterial space contained only
10 to the 0.6 million genomes

books beat bacteria, she said

but wait! it is too early to call
we were stingy with our genomes
only short bacterial genomes have
lengths of around 1 million bases
a more typical size is 5 million

this would give us 10 to the 3 million
possibilities for bacterial genomes and
now brave bacteria beat bold books
Borges cannot make his books
much larger but we can move
from bacteria to eukaryotes

Movement 2

small worms need genome sizes
of about 100 million letters while
mammals boast 3 billion letters
and flowering plants 100 billion

the entire observable universe
explores only a tiny fraction of books
but an even smaller fraction of genomes

we are forever out of resources, she joked

shall we move on?—why not

let us look at a simpler problem
let us study how evolution might
explore sequences of length 1000

now we are in a space containing
4 to the 1000 possible sequences
that is only 10 to the 600 points

much smaller than before but
still outstripping the total matter
in the observable universe

imagine a population of cells
each cell contains one sequence
when a cell divides a copy of
the sequence is made and each
daughter cell inherits one copy

whenever a copy is made
there is a chance of mutation
most copies are not perfect
they contain some mistakes

single letter substitutions
are called point mutations

in the beginning each cell
starts with a random sequence
we assume that the sequences
affect the rate of cell division

we call this rate "fitness"
each sequence entails a fitness

all sequences are aligned in space
nearest neighbors differ by one letter

since each sequence has a fitness
we can imagine a fitness landscape
arising over this sequence space

our fitness landscape is a mountain range
an assembly of peaks, ridges, valleys, plains
in a sumptuous plenitude of 1001 dimensions

the population explores that terrain
fitter sequences reproduce more rapidly
and leave more offspring while less fit ones
reproduce more slowly and are left behind

the population daringly moves upward
on mountain slopes toward summits

what view would it be standing on a
mountain top in 1001 dimensions!

depending on the mutation rate
and the shape of the landscape
evolution could find high peaks
but may never reach the top

it may never find the best match
of two people in want of each other
it may never attain the very peak
of harmonious existence

the best sequence is the global optimum
which glistens over the roof of the world
evolution may never attain that peak
but it could steadily improve on sequences
and find some reasonably good solutions

when a cell divides the genome is copied
mutations can occur in this process
we can consider a fixed probability
for each letter to be copied incorrectly
this probability is called mutation rate

there is an interesting relationship between
the sequence length and the mutation rate:
if the product of the two is less than one
then adaptation for higher fitness is possible

after leaving the courtyard they had been
slowly walking through narrow streets

history breathes authenticity, he thought
perhaps Mozart walked on those stones
when he encountered his servant, Joseph I
who had been sent to purchase a chicken
while the emperor's name was Joseph II

evolution can improve existing functions
but how does it discover new functions?

let us start with a population of sequences
but none has the function that is needed
we charge evolution with the task of finding
a new function which is not encoded by any
of the current sequences in the population

we assume that this new function improves
the reproductive rate of cells that contain it

since the function is not present at all
the first steps of the search are random
they cannot be guided by selection

initially evolution has only random drift
monkeys typing out text on type writers
until the first meaningful fragment arrives

if the new function is rare in space
then evolution will never find it

evolution can only discover new functions
that are so frequent that random sequences
instantiate them with high probability

once the population has such a sequence
evolution has a chance to improve on it
then the population can climb uphill
on a slope in the fitness landscape
but before that the population moves
aimlessly in a flat plain below the clouds

the great difficulty is to locate the peaks
in the vast flatlands of neutrality

do all new functions that evolution
has ever discovered have the property
that random sequences instantiate
them with high probability? she asked

maybe not—there is one other mechanism
which is called the regeneration process

imagine evolution has solved certain tasks
the cells already have a number of genes
which encode particular functions

now it could be that a new function
can be performed by an existing gene
if a few specific mutations occur there

then evolution could succeed as follows
it makes a copy of the existing gene
and starts neutral evolution of that copy

most of those random searches
lead further away from the target
rather than closer toward it
but discard all unsuccessful searches
keep regenerating the starting condition

after a manageable number of searches
there is success with high probability
the required number of searches
is a polynomial but not exponential
function of the sequence length

that gives us all the time in the world?
she asked

it does! time enough for life to unfold...

thus evolution can solve new problems
if it has solved similar problems already?

yes it follows

how does evolution solve the first problems?

the first problems must have been easy enough
for random sequences to get a grip on them
all subsequent problems were variations
on the themes of already solved problems

piano music transpired from an open window

they stopped and listened—then she said
Diabelli variations—of increasing complexity

3

he found himself in the library of Babel
it had not undergone gravitational collapse
but there seemed no way out of it either

for practical purposes he was
caught inside an event horizon
he walked around exploring

all rooms looked the same
not a single book was missing
not a single one was out of place

this was an entirely pristine library
maybe it was not open to the public
or it had an army of invisible librarians
who realigned all books after hours

or the library had no visitors
because people had given up
on the idea of finding anything
really useful in this domain

the more he thought about it
the more certainty he gained
that this last point explained
why the library lay deserted

it had a marketing problem
people no longer believed
in underlying reality

only extreme realists would
find their way into the library

in any case he was alone
which gave him the feeling
that he was on the right track

none of the books had any
writing on their covers

Movement 2

he wondered if he should
reach for a book and start
reading it or if he should
go to the next room hoping
that fortune would lead him
to a more interesting book
hope prevailed and he went on

in the next room he asked
himself the same question
and once again reached
the same conclusion

he executed this program
for a number of rooms

since all rooms were equal
how should he choose one
to examine his first book?
and in that room which
book should he choose?

was there a rational way to do this?

maybe he should go back
to the first room where he
started but would he find it?

then he realized there
was another problem

if this library contained every book
that was combinatorically possible
—as he assumed—then there was
really no chance that he could find
a book with something useful in it

hoping to learn something
by reading random books
in this library was irrational

it was similar to staring
at a computer screen
that displayed white noise
and expecting that by pure
chance the noise would
assemble into a movie
that was mesmerizing

how strange! he thought
to find yourself in a place
that contains all books
and then deem it irrational
to read a single one...

to him libraries had always been
both amazing and intimidating

then suddenly to considerable
surprise he perceived a person
in one of the adjacent rooms
he was not alone after all!

had a movie started perchance?
or was there another realist?

first he was startled then overjoyed
because beyond doubt it was her!

she was leaning over a book
reading it with visible delight

when he entered the room
she turned holding the book
she seemed not in the least
surprised to see him here

look, she said, all books in this room
and in the next ones are this book
with small mutations

which book? he asked

this very one here, she replied

Movement 2

they are arranged such that nearest
neighbors differ by a point mutation

i am reading the book now
and i have reached the place
where we meet in the library

you were amazed to find me here
but did you not know in your heart
that i was a devoted realist too?
she said joyfully rebuking him

i was not surprised you were here
because i was reading in the book
that you were wandering around
deeming it irrational to read and
then you found me reading

as you can see it is not wrong
to pick up a book and read

tolle lege!

all the while it seemed to him
that she was just reading
from the book which she held

he stepped to her side and looked
over her shoulder into the book

she pointed to *this* place
we are exactly *here*, she said
how astonishing! he read
is it astonishing? she asked

obviously this book must exist here
because every book is in this library

this is true, he read

moreover it is written here
that i am reading the book
while we meet in the library

now it is clearly implied that
we are reading those lines together
she traced them with her finger

it is neither astonishing nor irrational
it is a *fait accompli*—do you agree?

i agree that the book must exist
but does the event have to occur?

in underlying reality events do not occur
they just exist, she replied patiently

there is no one dimensional flow of time
in those rooms, she said looking around
as if thereby confirming her statement

anything that feels like time passing here
is a projection because we are used to it

in underlying reality events just are
and time is spatial

in other words the event in which
we are now exists in the book
and for this very same reason
we are in the library right now

he was trying to untwist knots
that were forming in his mind

while he had always considered
himself a realist he had to admit
that she seemed even more at
home in the domain than he was

his admiration for her grew...

oh please, she said, can you
just stop that for one moment
can't you see that i am normal
the definition of "everybody"?

the statement struck him as contestable
but worthy of further examination...

moreover, she said interrupting his thoughts
let us better focus on what is before us:
it is the book which requires our attention

how much he loved the timbre and
the perpetual playfulness of her voice
whose beauty was beyond comparison
even when she was reprimanding him

she stopped reading looked at him
and made a gesture as giving up

in any case there are other issues
to be considered, she continued
i was delighted to read the book
but i do have some questions

why are there two realms in the book?
and who is the me in the other realm?
is it even me? are there two women?
or just one? one of them is me, right?

are you writing the book?

at first i surmised you were the author
but then i saw that both of our thoughts
were transparent—and some of my thoughts
were described with tolerable accuracy

the question is: who is writing the book?

who is writing any book? he said
for a book to exist in this library
nobody needs to have written it
like integers books just are

for a realist the activity of writing a book
amounts to taking it from the underlying
reality into the instantiated material world

in this library books wait to be written
when you ask who does the writing
a superficial answer is: the author
a better answer is: the author's life

her life includes all people she has met
all photons that have reached her eyes
all sounds that have touched her ears
all interactions she had with forces of nature
every encounter with underlying reality

she is interwoven in the universe
she cannot be separated from it
it is the entire trajectory who does
the writing of every single book
do you realize the implication?

he was refocused — she was pleased

i ask you: who instantiates the trajectory?
who lifts the trajectory into existence?

the answer is God, the act is creation
every single book is an act of creation
and God is the ultimate author

they were silent as they just realized
they had read the last few lines together

4

they rested under a tree whose
magnificent branches provided
shade against the afternoon sun

she had interrupted her work
and was delighted to spend
time with her beloved teacher

they had found a new topic
which truly fascinated him

she narrated

sensing that a breakthrough was near
he sat down under a peepul tree and
vowed not to rise until enlightenment was his

it was a full moon of spring

near the city of Gaya?

yes nearby

and he had taken some food?

yes from a woman called Sujata
she offered him rice cooked in milk
he accepted the meal breaking his fast

as soon as he had sat down
Mara who anticipated that
a momentous transformation
was now about to take place
rushed to the spot attempting
to prevent what was imminent

as a first temptation Mara paraded
three beautiful women before him
but the Buddha-to-be remained seated

next Mara hurled weapons against him
deadly arrows and flaming rocks

but he had emptied himself so much
that the weapons could not harm him
they turned into soft flowers

then Mara changed his tactic
he questioned Siddhartha's right
to do what he intended to do

Siddhartha touched the earth
who gave him the right to proceed

then Mara left

Siddhartha's meditation deepened
the peepul tree rained blossoms on him
finally when the morning star glittered
he broke through the shell of finite self

he awoke a Buddha a fully enlightened one
a Tathagata who has won the Truth

the event was of cosmic grandeur
all creatures rejoiced, overwhelming bliss
rooted him to the spot for seven days

time and again he slipped in and out of nirvana
experiencing annihilation of selfish desire

he could have left this world forever
but in him was a voice of compassion
an imperative to save countless others
and to share the glory he had seen

Mara returned with a last challenge
now that you have gained enlightenment
you should leave this world at once
there is no reason for you to stay

what you have experienced cannot be shared!
what you have learned cannot be taught!
what you have seen cannot be shown!

Movement 2

the argument was compelling but after a while
the Buddha announced: some will understand
Mara left to return when his time would come

the Buddha searched for his five friends
whom he had temporarily abandoned
he found them in the deer park of Varanasi

in this place he gave his first sermon
setting the wheel of dharma in motion
he revealed the four noble truths

may i summarize them for you, good teacher?

nothing would delight me more, he replied

the trees were releasing flowers
they seemed lighter than the air
in which they floated

the first truth is the fact of suffering

people desire happiness in their lives
but tend to find the very opposite

they search for what is good and joyful
but they encounter sorrow and defeat

life is change and never satisfies desire
everything that can change will change
and will eventually bring suffering

the second truth is the cause of suffering

not life itself is responsible for suffering
but the demands we make on life

the cause of suffering is selfish desire
people aim to satisfy selfish desires
but selfishness brings unhappiness

the third truth is there is a cure

once the reason for suffering is
understood it can be cured

the cure is extinction of selfish desire
when the fire of selfishness is quenched
when the mind is set free
you can enter a state of peace and joy
a state of wakefulness or nirvana

the fourth truth is that selfishness
can be extinguished by following
the eightfold path which is:

right understanding, right purpose
right speech, right conduct
right occupation, right effort
right attention, right meditation

the eight spokes of the wheel of dharma

the words were flowing from her
she could not conceal her excitement
the teacher too was carried along

when did you acquire this great wisdom?
did you study Buddhism before i came here?

she looked at him with penetrating eyes
she wanted to answer but her mind moved
she gazed upward through the branches
and saw the sky—there were no limits!

she got up resuming her speech

it was such a brilliant insight
a perfect analysis of human life
a clearly illuminated path
an open road to success

the yearning to seek what is good
is inherent in all beings but the
motivation must not be selfish

you cannot long for the good
in order to have it for yourself
the sad desire for ownership
is a recipe for certain defeat

selfishness is a confusion holding us back
it is the primary reason for failure

but once selfishness is removed
you become a force for the good
you become a Buddha
you become a savior of worlds

good teacher, do you follow
what i am trying to say?
my words are so inadequate

my light, i am listening to you
your words are exceedingly beautiful
but do not call me good for only God is good

you call me "light" and i may not
call you "good"? she mused

at this moment and throughout her life
she was pure humility, absence of any vanity

she continued

the key insight is the need to rout selfish desire
the path begins with examining the notion of self

know thyself!

if you find an image of self that prompts you
to act selfishly then realize it is an illusion

this self has no permanence, no relevance
the ignorant are trapped by it, the wise ignore it

the message resonates with what we have read
in the other book which calls for selfless action
we find similar ideas in different guises
the wise come to matching conclusions

the Buddha's teaching is optimistic

for suffering he used the word "*dukkha*"
meaning "out of joint" or "dislocated"
something is dislocated in human life

his word for desire was *"tanha"*
which means the selfish desire
to strive for private fulfillment

the Buddha said hold on to truth
be a lamp in the darkness
work on your salvation

he asked us not to accept blindly
what is presented by authority
instead he encouraged us to search
for ourselves and to find our own
conclusions after careful reflection

his teaching is an analysis of life
a loving and sincere attempt to help

the teacher said, the concept of
"anatta" has always confused me

she looked at him and replied
"anatta" means "not self"

we can gain a better understanding
of life by renouncing the notion of self

we are talking of the provisional self
which is a powerful manipulator

it is this provisional self that leads us
to unwanted desires and worries

this provisional self is an illusion
any notion of self that leads to
private cravings is an illusion

beyond this provisional self
there is still the certainty of
the one and true self which
we call God—this is my view

some of his disciples interpreted
nirvana as finding the true self
which is the same in every creature

Movement 2

i say nirvana is finding God

"*anatta*" for me does not mean "no soul"
although there are eminent disciples
who might explicate it as such

disciples? the teacher asked

... of the Buddha, she completed

she touched the tree which bore her witness
she was lost in memories of bygone times

the idea of your own personal soul
could be misleading for some people
because it makes us too important

then it is better to think of no personal soul
which could present the illusion of self

do you agree? she asked

i am trying to comprehend, he answered
you described nirvana as finding God
but i thought Buddha did not talk of God

he did not, he kept a noble silence

his reason was: if a man is shot with an arrow
and is in pain, would you pull out the arrow
or first explore who made it? who shot it?
and for what reason? and so on

his mission was to help people immediately

some petals had settled in her hair
she did not notice them

the teacher looked at her wonderingly
who are you? what are you?

in the forest was a fragrance of summer

she said, people are asked: who are you?
but the Buddha was asked: what are you?

they asked him are you a god? he said no
they asked him are you an angel? he said no
then what are you? he replied, i am awake

he was the one who had woken up

he asked us to go against the current
against the impulse of revenge and greed

hatred cannot destroy hatred
punishment does not end crime
only love can dissolve conflict

he taught: *you are what you think*
pain follows an evil thought
as joy follows a pure thought

those who are selfless meditate
they can rejoice in this life

make an island for yourself

aim your thoughts like an archer
make your mind one-pointed
a trained mind brings happiness

do not call out the flaws of others
but instead mend your own faults

good deeds can be done in this life
neither lotus flower nor sandalwood
come near the fragrance of the good

avoid the road to profit and pleasure
the immature go after false prestige
they do not understand the dharma
as the spoon does not taste the soup

but the wise understand the dharma
as the tongue does taste the soup

a good deed brings no remorse
a selfish deed brings sorrow

*if you follow the teaching
you live in joy with a serene mind
you call nothing your own
you purify your heart and rejoice*

*you live in freedom full of light
wisdom has stilled your mind
your thoughts are peaceful
you are free from illusion*

*having renounced the world
of appearance you find truth
with your senses at peace
you make all forests holy*

*do not seek to defeat others
be victorious over yourself*

*one moment of wisdom
one moment of dharma
is more than a whole life
without wisdom or dharma*

*no harm comes to those who do no harm
but if you hurt others you harm yourself
they who are pure in heart enter nirvana*

*first learn what is right then teach others
be a guide onto yourself then guide others*

*do not follow the ways of the world
like a sleepwalker—instead wake up!
become wise and give light to the world!*

*the Buddha the fully awakened one
is free from all desires and passions*

cultivate the good, purify your mind

*you cannot uphold the dharma
by talking about it, you must live it*

of all paths the eightfold is the best
of all truths the noble four are best
of mental states detachment is best
of human beings the illuminated is best

this is the path to purification of the mind
but all efforts must be made by you
i can only show you the way

all created things are transitory
while meditation brings wisdom

the good shine like tall mountains tops
who glisten above the world

if you find a wise, loving friend
walk with him all the way

she looked at her teacher
and then she pronounced

i have conquered myself
i live in purity and i know
that this body is my last

he was startled

the words had poured out of her
then she reflected and was silent
she sat down abruptly
the flowers fell from her hair

her eyes were lowered now
and were fixed on the earth

after forty years of teaching in India
the Buddha's body had grown old

he told his disciple Ananda:

this body is an ancient cart
it is creaking and groaning
it needs constant care to go on
only in meditation i find peace

Movement 2

Mara has recently reappeared
i asked him to rejoice because
soon this body will leave his realm

Ananda wept

the Buddha scolded him

of all people you must know
that I will never leave you

i am not my body
unlimited by my body
unlimited by my mind
i am infinite and measureless

i live in the dharma
i live in the teaching
which i have given you

the teaching is inside you
closer to you than your heart
the dharma will never die

the next day the Buddha
looked over the city of Vaishali

then he and his disciples entered
the mango grove of a follower
named Chunda the smith

Chunda prepared a meal for them
afterwards the Buddha's body was in pain

Chunda was terrified worrying there
may have been a poison in his meal

but the Buddha told Chunda:
there were only two meals in my life
that have exceptionally blessed me
the milk rice i received from Sujata
which gave me the strength to find
enlightenment under the peepul tree
and your meal which opens the gate
for my final entry into nirvana

they continued on the road to Kusinara
Ananda noticed that the Buddha's skin
was shining like gold—he told Ananda
this happens twice in a Buddha's life
when he first enters nirvana and
when he finally enters nirvana

when they reached Kusinara
he asked to send for the people

if they wanted to see him a last time
they had to come now
because he will shed his body
during the third watch of the night

many people came, individuals and families

in the end he was alone with his disciples
he was resting on the side in the lion posture

he asked them
does anyone still have a question?
they all were silent

his final words were: all things that come
into being must pass away—strive earnestly!

then he entered nirvana a last time

5

later in the afternoon
she continued her chores
there were still many hours
in this day until sunset

she loved to work in the open
as the shadows grew longer
and the air adopted the calm
fragrance of descending evening

she reflected on the words
of their conversation today
had she talked too much?

but he seemed so interested
and he had led them to the topic

why are those memories in her?
why does she have knowledge
of ancient teachings and events?

from which books or scenes
are her memories stirring?

could she distinguish between
what she had read in a book
and what she had experienced
in the manifested world?

what about her own thoughts?
she observed them arise
she watched them pass
she could let them disperse

silently she performed her work
among the growing shadows
the predominant state inside her
was of all-embracing compassion

anyone for the other shore?

she halted her work briefly
and looked at the village

the people there were busy
with those tasks that arrived
at the end of a laborious day

putting their children to bed
securing animals for the night

anyone for the other shore?

she was looking at the people
with that love in her eyes

she was grateful to them
for adopting her when she
had come from nowhere

unconditional cooperation
prevailed among them
and was even extended
to visitors who passed by

they had given her a small
unused piece of land which
she had turned into a garden

the teacher making fun of it
called it the garden of Eden
he liked to observe her efforts
which had a tendency to fail

yet children loved the berries
and women loved the herbs
there were some small trees
which occasionally bore fruit

everyone could come and take
freely whatever they wanted
one day the children had eaten
all berries even those that were unripe
but the next day there were new ones

Movement 2

once she experimented with bees
to make honey but unsuccessfully

the girls in the village adored her
some of the boys looked at her
as a particular one had long ago

her friends were the milkmaids
yet she was not one of them

she always aimed to assume
the lowest position in the village
she worked without getting tired
and she was a servant for all

although everyone respected her
it was not respect she cared for

she was like the air which was freely
available for all people to breathe
and asked for nothing in return

there was no design in her
to act in any particular way
she was one with nature
one with all, one with the One

all she did was natural
creation in her was flawless
this purity left her void
of differentiating features
she really was everybody
or nobody?—a shadow?

she was invisible in the space
where selfish desires marked
distinct niches for individuals

confusion she knew not
she wanted to teach others
to become unconfused too

she allowed herself little time to study
though reading was her favorite activity
her most cherished reward after work

she read the precious books at night
in her room to the light of a candle
or outside in the moonlight when
the ancient companion shone undimmed

❀ ❀ ❀

after this day's conversation
the teacher was deep in thoughts

he had often witnessed that
she had not only knowledge
but sincere comprehension

every learned book she read
she retained immediately

after only a single reading
she understood the central
message and even more

as previous teachers had said
you explain to her one wisdom
and she returns ten others

but today he was more puzzled
than on previous occasions

he went to the library of the village
which had a modest collection
he searched for books on Buddhism
but found none—not a single one

6

we have discussed evolution as a
search process in which populations
travel over fitness landscapes

fitness landscapes are mountain
ranges in high dimensional spaces
they arise when genetic sequences
are assigned reproductive rates

the fittest types are represented
by the highest peaks which are
towering over the roof of the world

ridges might connect those peaks
or they face off over deep valleys

there is a point on earth where
two 8000-meter mountains
face each other over a river valley

they performed a random walk
in the city slowly drifting toward
a museum she wanted him to see
he seemed unusually focused today

populations move over the rugged
terrain attempting to climb uphill

their motion is propelled
by mutation and selection
their fuel is reproduction
energy comes from the sun

if the fitness landscape is fixed
we talk of constant selection

we may also encounter evolution
on landscapes that are changing
they could change because of the
environment or as a consequence
of temporal or spatial variation

but they can also change because
of the movement of the population

as the population moves by evolution
peaks can become taller, valleys deeper
or peaks turn to valleys, or valleys to peaks

the concept here is that fitness
which is reproductive success
depends on the relative abundance
of various types in the population

relative abundance is frequency
we move from constant selection
to frequency-dependent selection

a trait could do well when rare
but badly when common
or a trait does badly when rare
but well when common

the idea opens for us the door
to access the brave new world
of evolutionary games

their walk led through a park
the afternoon was pleasant
yet there were bursts of wind
occasionally dispersing her hair

this reminded him of something
perhaps an image of poetry?
but for now it remained hidden
in the museum of his thoughts

what kind of games? she asked

Movement 2

everything is a game, he replied
life has a fondness for games

distinct games are staged by evolution
one of them is the eternal contest
between cooperation and defection
between good and evil

is cooperation always good and
defection always bad? she asked

maybe not always, he admitted
but often cooperation is desirable
while defection is exploitative

cooperation seeks the well-being of all
while defection is self-centered

cooperation means paying a cost
for someone else to have a benefit
while defection avoids paying a cost
and thus provides no benefit

in the world of natural selection
individuals compete with each other
for space, resources or partners

it seems, she said, there is no option
for traits to be selected which leads
one individual to help a competitor

precisely, he answered, all individuals
participate in the struggle for survival

competition opposes cooperation
natural selection prefers defectors
because they avoid paying a cost

cooperators reduce their fitness
by paying costs to help others

yet cooperation occurs in nature
she said, and is even abundant

then we must ask, he replied
how can selection favor cooperation?
how can competition lead to cooperation?

cooperation is not only ubiquitous
one can argue that cooperation is
the master architect of evolution

whenever evolution makes great discoveries
some form of cooperation is involved

the emergence of the first cell required cooperation
of different molecules: DNA, RNA, lipids, proteins

it needed a coming together and a
staying together of such compounds

coming together and staying together
are specific tools in the repertoire of
evolutionary construction

cells are cooperative aggregates of genes

bacteria can cooperate in harvesting food
which they encounter outside of the cell

at a cost they produce enzymes
to break down available food
to import the smaller pieces

cooperators produce enzymes which
benefit themselves and others locally

defectors do not produce the enzymes
thereby they save costs and live off
the generosity of nearby cooperators

bacteria sometimes feed each other
precious nutrients or they cooperate
in forming large structures

they cooperate in filaments where some
cells die to supply others with nitrogen

or they cooperate by division of labor
some cells develop the ability to swim
to hold the aggregate in a certain place
while other cells become reproductives

evolution of multi-cellularity is
based on cooperation among cells
breakdown of such cooperation
destroys multi-cellular organisms

social insects and other animal societies
are structured around cooperation
workers raise the offspring of the queen

humans often cooperate with each other
but not always—and this is our weakness

they stood in front of a museum
here it is, she said, shall we go in?
gladly and curiously he accepted

evolution is not just competition
evolution is not only a brutish fight
evolution is also cooperation
cooperation is a fundamental principle

the traditional view is one of competition
survival of the fittest, everyone for himself
cell against cell, organism against organism
man against man, woman against woman

an unbroken line of winners connects us
to the origin of life four billion years ago
keep fighting! keep winning!

but is this really all of evolution?
is it that bleak? is history so dark?

admission to the museum was free
a museum is a kind of public good
a house of cooperation, she explained

but the other view is that cooperation
is a truly important aspect of evolution
he continued, there is abundant scope
for helping others, for working together

in this view our ancestors were those
who helped each other
who received help from others

then an unbroken line of cooperators
connects us to the origin of life, she said
and this is a more pleasing perspective

fortunately there was no inconvenient
struggle for survival in the museum
it was not as empty as the library
but it was not overcrowded either

unlike the deserted library of Babel
this museum evidently enjoyed
the ability to attract some visitors

people were respectfully engaged
in the admiration of great artifacts
which had crystallized over time

people cooperated with each other
by giving space, by speaking quietly

we harvest the fruits of cooperation
long in the making, she commented

imagine a museum, she continued
where all objects of art are assembled
that humans have ever composed
the museum gives us an evolutionary
trajectory of all creative offerings

someone could be your guide
in that museum moving you
along through the centuries
laid out in corridors and rooms

Movement 2

she led him into certain directions
he followed her without hesitation
the museum had a vast collection
seemingly covering every period

i have been here before, he thought
but with her everything looks different

they entered the Babylonian section

one version of history is: all these
civilizations flourished for some time
they held on while they were strong
and suppressed others, eventually
they grew weak and were destroyed

they looked at items in the room
she pointed to a text which seemed
to translate some cuneiform tablets

climb with me the stone staircase
more ancient than the mind can imagine
approach the Eanna temple sacred to Ishtar
walk with me on the wall of great Uruk
see the lush gardens, orchards, temples

the Babylonian monk Shin-Leqi-Unninni
writing in 1200 BC is inviting his readers
to visit a city which existed long ago
it was as impossible for them to visit Uruk
as it is for us today, she explained

the epic describes the king
who had seen everything
who had experienced all emotions

read of Gilgamesh how he suffered all
how he accomplished all

i love the part when Gilgamesh traverses
in complete darkness the tunnel which
the sun takes under the earth after setting
in the west to return to the east, he said
Gilgamesh has twelve hours to emerge
on the other side before the sun enters

oh you heroes! she said, brave old world
and brave new world of such heroes!

he felt understood

i think Shin-Leqi-Unninni, he continued
is the first author in human history

is that so? she wondered, let's go back!

she walked out of the room
they traversed several rooms until
she saw what she had been seeking

she went to a cabinet and read
the Sumerian poet Enheduanna
who lived 2200 BC is the earliest writer
in history whose name is recorded

daughter of king Sargon she was
high priestess of the goddess Inanna
and of the moon god Nanna

she created the forms of poetry
psalms and prayers that were used
throughout the ancient world
her work led to the development
of the genres recognized today

through the Babylonians her art
influenced both the Homeric epics
and the psalms of the Hebrew Bible
from there her voice reached the
hymns of the early Christian church

Movement 2

that is truly impressive, he said
i must admit i did not know of her

there are many things between heaven
and earth you do not know, she said

suddenly he remarked in a manner
as if revealing a decisive deduction
wait! you said, let's go back
but we have not passed here before
we did not come this way

i meant in time, she replied
let's go back in time
in this museum we can move
both in time and in space

then you knew of Enheduanna?

yes, i did

and i am sure you realize that
the goddess Innana of whom
she was priestess is the same
as Ishtar the patron goddess
of the Eanna temple in Uruk

they walked on

already then Eanna, queen of heaven
was associated with the evening star

later she was loved by the Assyrians
who made her the highest goddess
of their own exalted pantheon

in sequence she became
the phoenician goddess Astoreth
the greek goddess Aphrodite
and the roman goddess Venus

goddess of beauty and of love
love in its noble and basic aspects
wife of Vulcanus and of Anchises
to whom she bore Aeneas

suddenly she lowered her eyes

and finally he remembered the verse
he had been searching for in the park
dederatque comam diffundere ventis[10]

you have no face of a mortal! he thought

Caesar and Augustus claim ancestry to her
asserting an unbroken line, she added

later they stood in another room
before an ancient object which was
rolled out of silver bars, of tin
of stubborn brass of solid gold

he gazed at it in rising disbelief
which catered to her amusement

with deliberate calm she explicated
here we can see the sun, the moon
and all the stars, two cities of people
a wedding in one, a siege of the other
ploughing of a field, reaping the harvest
a vineyard and a farm of sheep

i love sheep, she said
interrupting the ekphrasis

a herd of straight-horned cattle
here is dancing to my delight
around we have the entire ocean

it is a mandala showing the cosmos
sun and moon shine at the same time
the moon is a perfect circle, these facts
point to a cosmological understanding

i trust you know this shield?

Movement 2

he was silent

it was made by Hephaestus, she said
who was Aphrodite's husband

but surely this can only be...

he could not formulate his concerns
as she led him away in time and space

they meandered through the greco-roman world
others carve finer statues and produce greater art
but your fate, o roman, is to rule the world

he wondered what if the world
was not ruled by power and greed
was not ruled by malice and anger
but was ruled by loving kindness?

what if people could find her?
no law of nature precluded that state
but how could it be reached?

it was a recurrent dream
imagine the form of the good
not as a servant but as a ruler
a clearly visible beacon of light

but how did we get here?
was the museum changing
as they moved through it?

she stopped and looked at him
it seems to me there are aspects
of history i do not need to learn
i recall them as if i am part of them

after this revelation he was even
more perplexed about her than before

7

they had continued in the museum
reaching medieval Christianity

the room presented as a church
there was tranquility and peace
they saw statues, glass windows
altar pieces, a baptismal fountain

they sat down and talked quietly
not daring to raise their voices

imagine evolution had been discovered
in the middle ages or even before

it would not have posed a problem
for the theology or the philosophy
of Augustine or of Thomas Aquinas

for Augustine a spiritual interpretation
of Genesis was acceptable as we know
and Aquinas said everything that is done
by nature must be traced back to God

they were silent, then he continued

yet the first view of evolution
as formulated in the 19th century
had a philosophical problem

if evolution is only competition
why should we love our neighbor?
if all aspects of evolution are selfish
why should humans be unselfish?

cynics tend to reply that humans
are not unselfish and never will be
but we want to move beyond that

a new view of evolution solves the problem:
evolution is not only competition
it is both competition and cooperation

Movement 2

from the dawn of time evolution included
cooperation—the quest for cooperation is
as old and fundamental as evolution itself
the call for cooperation is ubiquitous

then we can talk of natural cooperation
in addition to natural selection, she said

yes! he replied, i completely agree
everything inside him approved of her

we have to solve the following puzzle:
selection tends to oppose cooperation
if that is the case we must wonder:
how can cooperation ever succeed?

we find that cooperation can evolve
if certain mechanisms are in place
there are five such mechanisms
they are interaction structures

but let us first see how cooperation
loses without such a mechanism

cooperators pay a cost to benefit others
defectors pay no cost and give no benefit

imagine a game between two people
for example between you and me

there are two crucial parameters
which we call "benefit" and "cost"

benefit and cost are numbers
they take numerical values

the rules of our game are
benefit is greater than cost
and cost is greater than zero

if you cooperate you incur a cost
and i receive the benefit

if you defect you have no cost
and i receive no benefit

in the game we are supposed
to decide simultaneously

if both of us cooperate we both
receive benefit minus cost

if you cooperate and i defect
your payoff is minus cost
and mine is plus benefit

if you defect and i cooperate
your payoff is plus benefit
and mine is minus cost

if we both defect we get zero

if we play the game just once
what would you do?

what would you do? she asked in return

she thought, i would maximize our payoff
he thought, i would maximize her payoff
together they said, i would cooperate

this is not what i hoped to show, he said
this is not what rational players do

so called "rational" players, she replied
because selfishness is not rational

but i know, she said, we have to imagine
the game happens between selfish players
who seek to maximize their own payoff

you are right, he said, the payoff
should be interpreted as indicating
that which players really want

if players have additional objectives
they should be written into the payoff

fine, she said, let us be selfish
assume the payoffs signify what we "want"
she signed inverted commas with her fingers

Movement 2

in that case, she said, it is like this:
if i assume you cooperate then i maximize
my payoff when i defect because benefit
is greater than benefit minus cost

if i assume you defect then again
i maximize my payoff when i defect
because zero is greater than minus cost

if you analyze the game in the same way
we both defect and get zero payoff

this is a pity because had we cooperated
we would have received a greater payoff

now i have analyzed the game using
what you might call "rationality"
—again inverted commas

it has led us to the Nash equilibrium
though we are still in the middle ages
he remarked

do not underestimate them, she said
shall we move to the renaissance?

walking toward that period, he said
i can tell you an anecdote about Nash

someone told his friends a riddle:
the poor have it, the rich need it
it is greater than God
it is more evil than the devil
if you eat it you will die

do you know the answer already?

i do, she replied, it is so obvious

some of his friends also knew it at once

a physicist who would win a Nobel prize
—for solving another riddle—took an hour

but Nash sent his answer the next day writing
"first i thought you were posing a mathematical
puzzle then i noted a verbal answer was possible
figuratively one can say: the poor have nothing,
the rich need nothing; and the following religious
statements are popular: nothing is greater than
God nothing is more evil than the devil"

very elegant and rational! she was amused

then she pointed to a fresco in the room
which they had just entered and exclaimed
the Athenian academy! Raphael's masterpiece!
Plato is pointing to heaven, Aristotle to earth
all philosophers are assembled around them

surprised he gazed at the fresco whose
sudden appearance stunned him

here is Heraclitus, she pointed out
you can never step into the same river twice
all is change, all is in flux, all is becoming

here Parmenides: out of nothing nothing comes
whatever is is, whatever is not can never be
reality is ungenerated, unchanging, indestructible

important forerunners for Plato, do you agree?
she asked him with one of her smiles

it was lost on him for now
not the smile but the philosophy
because he was still puzzled...

there is one figure that looks at us
can you spot him? or her? she said

some art historians interpret her
as Hypatia who was a mathematician
a neoplatonist philosopher living
in Alexandria in the fourth century
she was pagan but greatly admired
by both pagan and Christian students
she was killed by a Christian mob

Movement 2

she was seen as a martyr for philosophy
against Christianity but later her story
was mixed up with that of Saint Catherine
of Alexandria who was a Christian martyr

much of this was lost on him for now
instead he focused on the inexplicable
presence of the fresco in the museum

i am sure the original of this painting
is in the Vatican, he said, is this a copy?
why would a museum display a copy?
in what kind of museum are we here?

shall we continue our games? she proposed

sure, if you like

he decided to solve the mystery
of the museum at a later time

instead of using rationality
let evolution solve the game

imagine a population of cells
some cooperate some defect
thereby they accumulate payoff
which is reproductive success

since defectors avoid paying a cost
but all cells receive the same benefit
defectors earn more than cooperators
defectors outcompete cooperators
in the end all cells will be defectors

in this example natural selection reduces
the average fitness of a population

a population of cooperators has highest fitness
a population of defectors has lowest fitness

natural selection found the Nash equilibrium

now let us explore how natural selection
could eventually smile on cooperation

there are five mechanisms
the first one uses repetition
it is called direct reciprocity

most interactions among humans
occur in the context of repetition
we interact repeatedly with friends
colleagues and family members
we go to the same restaurant
we visit the same stores

if the game is repeated then defection
is not the only Nash equilibrium in town
cooperation can become an equilibrium
if we use a strategy to incentivize it

we can do this in a very simple way
i could say: i start with cooperation
i cooperate as long as you cooperate
if you defect once i will defect forever
this strategy is called "grim"

it is very sad and punitive, she said

yes it is, furthermore it is a bad strategy
one mistake destroys cooperation forever

but still if you know i am playing grim
you maximize your payoff by cooperating

if the game is repeated often enough
and we don't know when it ends, she said

precisely! he exclaimed

you could say there is a certain
probability for another round
if that probability is large enough
then cooperation makes sense

she said, i guess the probability has
to exceed cost divided by benefit

did you just calculate that?

if grim is bad what is a good strategy?
she asked side-stepping his question

exactly! that is what we want to know
what is a good strategy for cooperation?

a strategy is a function that specifies
for any sequence of past outcomes
the probability to cooperate next round

probabilities are real numbers
we are in the realm of continuous infinity

if we admit only rational probabilities
for rational players then we are back
to discrete infinity, she offered

ha-ha that is true!

do you find infinity beautiful? he asked

very beautiful, she answered

the greeks considered it an imperfection
they were surprised when Plato proposed
that the good was infinite

were they? she wondered now distracted
by the pictures they saw in the new room

Titian, she announced looking around
then walking to a particular painting
she said: Venus Anadyomene

rising from the sea she is born fully grown
do you see a trace of red in her hair?

they looked at the painting

did he compare her in the painting
with her standing before it?

after some time she recalled the present
you were saying something about strategies
we were talking about strategies...
oh yes...but wait...we must not miss

she made a few steps to an adjacent room

Sandro... Botticelli...

they now looked at Primavera

dressed for a change, she remarked

do you see her golden sandals?
i love the flowers on the forest floor
they are many different species
look at the fruits in the trees
Mercury is dispersing the clouds

more has been written about
that painting than of any other

then she turned to the right
and saw *The Birth of Venus*

over there getting dressed
she said apologetically

the winds are blowing her ashore

she touched her hair
was it ever that long?

the wind is raining flowers
but none are settled in her hair
the coastline abuts the ocean of truth
the hora of spring is bringing her cloak
she is hovering over spots of gold

was Venus born in spring? he asked

it was always spring then, she affirmed

why are the winds male and female?

Zephyr and Aura, the latter a gentle breeze

is it the same model for Venus in both paintings?

this has been debated for centuries, she replied

standing between the two paintings she asked
if a carpenter makes a new table
does he make it after a broken or a perfect one?

he would use a perfect one

and what is the most perfect table
for a philosopher who is a realist? she asked

the Platonic form of a table, he replied

she nodded

she moved to another picture in the room
he also did one of my favorite annunciations
the lines are so clear, the angel is on his knees

he did not interrupt her contemplation
he noticed that she was very moved here

after some time she proposed
shall we return to cooperation?

he hesitated

don't worry, she encouraged him
all serious efforts are precious to me
every scientist longs to be an artist
because only art gives uniqueness

moreover i have the feeling there
are two stories unfolding in parallel

we were looking for strategies, he said
that help us to incentivize cooperation
somewhat better than grim is tit-for-tat

tit-for-tat starts with cooperation
it responds to cooperation with cooperation
it responds to defection with defection

tit-for-tat holds up a mirror and enforces
that you play against your own previous move

tit-for-tat does well if there are no errors
but it performs poorly when errors occur
it retaliates if a player defects by mistake
it re-retaliates after a retaliation

in a long game with errors two tit-for-tat players
perform as poorly as if they were flipping a coin
in each round for deciding what to do

in order to evaluate the success of a strategy
in the repeated game three key questions are:
how does the strategy perform against itself?
how does it perform against all-defect?
how does it perform against all-cooperate?

all-defect is the strategy that always defects
while all-cooperate always cooperates

i like unconditional cooperation, she said

tit-for-tat cannot be exploited by all-defect
if the game is sufficiently long
but two tit-for-tat players do not achieve
full cooperation in a world of errors

an improvement is generous-tit-for-tat
this strategy starts with cooperation
it cooperates if you have cooperated
it sometimes cooperates if you have defected

generous-tit-for-tat has a parameter
denoting the probability to forgive
if that probability is not too high
then it is stable against all-defect

but the higher the probability to forgive
the higher the payoff between two players
using generous-tit-for-tat: you want to be
as forgiving as possible but not more so

consider four strategies: all-defect, tit-for-tat,
generous-tit-for-tat, all-cooperate

Movement 2

if in a society everyone uses always-defects
tit-for-tat has a chance to initiate cooperation
it is a good catalyst for starting cooperation

but once cooperation thrives tit-for-tat
loses quickly to strategies that can forgive
generous-tit-for-tat emerges and takes over
this is evolution of forgiveness in action

but if everyone uses generous-tit-for-tat
another instability arises: all-cooperate
gains the same payoff as generous-tit-for-tat
it advances by drift as neutral mutants do

once the population uses all-cooperate
it is an invitation for all-defect to come in
consequently cooperation breaks down
we have endless cycles of war and peace

the emphasis is not on equilibrium
the realization is: nothing is fully stable
there exists no cooperative utopia
there is no society that is entirely lost
it is always an up and a down

all is in flux, she said

is that some greek philosophy? he asked

she looked at him, but forgave quickly

the key question is: how much time
do we spend in a cooperative state?
we must aim to design structures
that make cooperation last once
it is established and to rebuild it
quickly once it is destroyed

win-stay, lose-shift is another strategy
that can stabilize cooperation

it works according to the principle:
repeat your move if you are doing well
change your move if you are doing badly

two such players cooperate with each other
because they can correct mistakes

against all-defect the strategy attempts
to cooperate in every other round
but it can still fight off invasion
if benefit is greater than twice the cost

the advantage of win-stay, lose-shift is
that it is not neutral with all-cooperate
it will discover—accidentally—that it
can dominate unconditional cooperation

do i like that feature? she wondered

after the Baroque she said

in this world of repeated games we get
cooperation using appropriate strategies
they need to be generous in some sense
they have to be willing to forgive mistakes
but they also need to be able to defend
themselves when being attacked

this gives rise to a world of strategic
cooperation but is this real altruism?
is the behavior motivated by love?
how does the quest lead to love?
and what about sacrificial behavior?
who are the real winners in the game?
is a saint a winner or a loser?

please hold those questions for now
in your mind or in your heart since
the answers may emerge over time

they reached a gallery of impressionists
he looked at the pictures from a distance
while she walked from one to the next

Movement 2

the room spoke to him of summer, of nature
of sea side, of rivers upon which time flowed
you can never step into the same river twice
had he missed something in the renaissance?

then he looked at the pictures no more
the interaction with her i value infinitely
she constitutes infinite payoff for me
and for all who are blessed to know her

how does she do it?

we want the good, we infinitely want the good
if she upholds the good then all she wants is good
and thus we want to do everything she wants
following her constitutes infinite payoff for me
but why infinite? because the good is infinite

why this sensation of good in her presence?
because she brings you before the absolute
because she promises a new world order

her love is unbounded transcending spacetime
her selflessness silences all selfishness in you
leaves you completely in the state of anatta
knowing her makes you free as the wind

love is desire for that which you have not
but true love makes you absolutely free

a saint wins in the end because her payoff
is the true payoff of all others

8

by your wish we have begun
to study the other approach
would you like to summarize
what you have read recently?

my teacher, i delight in the books
your kindness enables me to read
great wisdom i encounter in them

they were gaining a mountain slope
rising steeply from the ocean of truth
which was visible between the trees

this then is my poor recollection
of the learned words i have read

centuries after the Buddha had walked
the paths of India, in a distant country
the teaching was favored by the court
but seen as a tool to secure prosperity

the role of the priests was to offer
prayers for the emperor and the nation
and many of them were striving
for worldly rewards, for rank and power

there were also pious men and women
who acted out of genuine compassion
and who followed the Buddha's teaching

they built lodgings for the clergy
shelters for homeless and hospitals
where priests practiced medicine

there was a monk who at young age
was already the disciple of a priest

after his ordination he withdrew
lamenting the transience of life
and the decline of the dharma
he retreated into the mountains

remaining in solitude he lived
as a hermit for many years

his poetic offerings are moving
the three realms of desire, form
and formlessness are filled with
suffering and nowhere is peace
how pitiful are all living beings

life is a breeze which cannot be stayed
our bodies are dew which soon disappears

alone he searched for what he called
the unsurpassed and supreme truth
his efforts led him to comprehend
that a unified teaching was needed

he applied for the emperor's permission
to travel and study at the T'ien-t'ai school

he brought their ideas back to his country
he founded a monastery on his mountain
he established the noble Tendai school
which evokes wisdom of the Lotus Sutra

the aim was to show that all teachings
of the Buddha can be unified into one
single system without any contradiction

the pinnacle of Tendai philosophy is
the doctrine of original enlightenment

all human experience is based
on the perception of dualities:
good and evil, birth and death,
self and other, young and old,
male and female, mind and body

yet those dualities are only
present in provisional reality
they are temporary divisions
of what was one originally
of what will be one again
of what is one in truth

they had reached a beautiful spot
with unimpaired views over the ocean

following the coastline north do you see
the mountain in the blue distance? he asked

i can see it, she said

do you know of it?

i have seen it before but its name
or significance is unrevealed to me

it is the mountain which elevates
the emperor's palace to heaven

i did not know that an emperor
is ruling our temporal realm
we must sincerely pray for him
because it is easy to go wrong
if you wield power over people

the teacher looked at her in surprise
there is no emperor and no empress
there have not been for a long time
the palace is empty—she was silent

they sat down under the trees
which shaded against the midday sun

the teacher had brought food
he offered it to her with tea
she accepted both gratefully

Movement 2

then she added with a smile
but my food is to do the will
of my Father who is in heaven

yet your Father still wants you
to consume your daily portion
which comes from Him, he replied

if you eat this bread you will be
hungry again but if you consume
the food that i am indicating
you will hunger no more, she said

are you ever hungry? he asked

i am often hungry, she replied

he blessed the bread and they ate

afterwards she continued

the principle of non-duality applies to
the absolute being and the absolute realm
both can only be perceived if we break
through the perception of duality

a great teacher of the Tendai school remarked:
as my body is Buddha and Buddha is my body
so this world is perfect bliss and perfect bliss
is this world

it is a wonderful realization: enlightenment
can be achieved by ordinary people
a possibility of buddhahood is in everyone

non-duality also clarifies our view of eternity
when we see eternity as endless continuation
of time we do not understand it

when we transcend the phenomenon of time
we find eternity in the present moment

in the other book you gave me i read
eternity and the present moment are one
there is no distinction between beginning
middle and end; the first instant of thought
is the eternally abiding unchanging thought

she looked toward the horizon of the world

as on the great ocean the waves of yesterday
today and tomorrow are one in substance
so the thoughts of the three worlds
past, present, and future are one thought

this is the teaching of the eternal present
the eternity of the absolute moment

we are asked to transcend
the duality of life and death
life and death are of one substance
emptiness and being are non-dual
the absolute realm is unity

renounce attachment to dualistic perception
gain awareness of monistic essence

some have argued that this teaching is
a crowning achievement of Buddhist philosophy

do you agree, my good teacher?

they looked out over the great ocean of truth
its eternal waves of past, present, and future

whatever is is, what is not can never be

they perceived the world as perfect bliss
theirs was a gift of a transcendent harmony
surpassing all human passion and desire

would you reveal the one episode
in the book that has moved you
more than the others? he asked

suddenly her penetrating eyes were on his
and they revealed considerable surprise
after a moment of what could have been
perceived as mutual recognition she said

in the sutra we learn of a young woman
who is the daughter of a king
she is wise beyond her age
she knows the intentions of all beings
she has the power of recollection
she keeps memories of all buddhas
she is capable of deep meditation
she can discern all teachings
she has surpassing eloquence
she thinks of others as her children

her faculties are sharp, her virtues perfect
her explanations subtle, her thoughts merciful
she has a harmonious mind in a state of bliss

when encountering the Buddha
she offers him a pearl which signifies her life
the Buddha accepts the offer
and at once she attains full enlightenment

9

they stood in front of Van Gogh's
painting of the Good Samaritan

it is amazing how he saw the world
despite his suffering or because of it
he painted this picture in his cell
in a hospital in the south of France
he was inspired by a work of Delacroix

the Good Samaritan was not motivated
by direct reciprocity, would you agree?

i agree

what we see here is not the first round
of a repeated game, she continued

i guess it is not

then people can also cooperate
in situations that are not repeated

of course

there may be few Good Samaritans
among us but many people want
to help if it is not too inconvenient

this brings us to the next mechanism
which is called indirect reciprocity

here my behavior towards you depends
on what you have done to others

indirect reciprocity arises when interactions
occur in the presence of interested audiences

we live in the audience of God, she thought

direct reciprocity utilizes repetition
indirect reciprocity uses reputation

Movement 2

two other flavors of reciprocity
are downstream and upstream
downstream reciprocity means
i help you and someone helps me
upstream reciprocity means i help
you and you help someone else

both are misdirected acts of gratitude
in one you are thanked by someone
who did not benefit by what you did
in the other you thank someone
for something that another did

upstream reciprocity means a good deed
triggers a sequence of other good deeds
upon receiving help you enter a state
which make you cooperate with others

if each recipient of cooperation pays
it forward to more than one person
then upstream reciprocity leads to
an explosive epidemic of goodness

she got very excited
this is what we want for the world

true!

shall we leave the museum now
to go out into the world?

so soon?

there is a world outside the museum

my world is where you are, he thought

we won't leave art behind
we take the memories with us
and we find new ones outside

they drifted toward the door and
then passed through it into the city

outside he turned to look back
i must return and examine the objects
we have seen today, he thought

it was a pleasant summer evening
the roads were closed for traffic
and populated by pedestrians

perceiving music in the distance
they headed into that direction

upstream reciprocity is not a mechanism
it requires a mechanism for cooperation

if there are those that can be triggered
to cooperate and those that cannot
then natural selection favors the latter

but if the ability to be triggered comes
with a reputation that is liked by others
then indirect reciprocity can endorse
its upstream companion

downstream reciprocity on the other hand
is an integral part of indirect reciprocity
if i help you after you helped someone
then my behavior towards you depends
on what you have done to others
and this is precisely indirect reciprocity

they reached the open air concert
they saw orchestra and conductor
the music carried over the crowd
it was Mahler's 7th symphony

for a brief moment he thought
Mahler himself was conducting
what a transcendent conductor
what a magic midsummer night

music can make us joyful and sad
it can be part of a healing process
it can illuminate great moments
or induces solemn acceptance

Movement 2

music removes internal contradiction
it enables you to see who you are
it focuses you on what is essential

see what music accomplishes here
people are joyful, solemn, happy, sad,
exhilarated, moved... they are alive!
they are suspended in the moment

perhaps music helps to trigger
the chain reaction of indirect reciprocity?
see how the world is transformed!

for him too the world was transformed
but not only by Mahler's genius alone
though he was a transcendent composer

for him she was the music
she was the night
she was the midsummer night
she was the one focal point from
which all love, beauty, and goodness
flowed into the veins of civilization

when the movement had finished
there was an intermission

she said, let us find a quiet place
to continue writing our score

i know where we can go, he replied

they moved toward the university
they slipped into its courtyard
where roses were still in bloom

all doors stood open in this night
busts of eminence were looking on
Boltzmann, Schrödinger, Zeilinger

how appropriate, she said

indirect reciprocity is a mechanism
enabling evolution of cooperation

in one setting of indirect reciprocity
cooperation leads to a good reputation
defection leads to a bad reputation

others consider your reputation
when deciding to help you or not

does the samaritan help because
the injured has a good reputation?

i guess the reputation of the victim
was unknown to the samaritan

a key aspect of the theory is what to do
when someone's reputation is unknown
would you help a stranger?

winning strategies help strangers
their opening move is cooperation
let us call this property "hopeful"

hope makes you cooperate with a newcomer
hope advances a positive perspective on life

winners are not only hopeful
but they are also generous and forgiving

i commend those features, she said

"generous" means you let others have more
you do not insist on winning every encounter
you win by being a partner not an opponent

forgiveness allows you to rebuild trust
with those who have failed you

forgiveness enable them to come back into life
you appeal to the good that prevails in all beings

a key question of indirect reciprocity is:
if you meet someone with a bad reputation
should you cooperate or defect?

Movement 2

indirect reciprocity relies on the idea
that defectors do not receive cooperation
but whenever you choose to defect
you could harm your own reputation

one way to solve the issue is introducing
a social norm which prescribes as follows:
if you meet a defector you must defect
and this does not harm your reputation

there are problems with that norm
because it is vulnerable to deception

i could try to make you believe that
the other person has a bad reputation
and then my own defection with him
is justified although i am the defector

strategies of indirect reciprocity have
an action rule and a social norm

the action rule specifies how to act
that is whether to cooperate or not
given the other person's reputation
and possibly considering your own

the social norm specifies how to evaluate
interactions that occur between others

a simple social norm is the following:
cooperation leads to a good reputation
defections leads to a bad reputation

a more complex norm also depends
on the reputation of the recipient
defecting with a good recipient
could lead to a bad reputation
defecting with a bad recipient
could lead to a good reputation

even more complicated norms
include the reputation of the donor
you could evaluate it differently if a
good or bad person refuses to help

of course "good" and "bad"
are simple labels in that game
reputation need not be binary
it could be described by more
intricate variables which count
how often a person has helped
and in what circumstances

it is possible that the games
of indirect reciprocity provided
the crucial selection pressure
that caused the cerebral
expansion in human evolution

the games are cognitively demanding
people need to follow what happens
to them and between others

they monitor the social network and
ask who does what to whom and why

indirect reciprocity requires storage
of information and strategic thinking
it requires language

the biologist David Haig remarked
for direct reciprocity you need a face
for indirect reciprocity you need a name

among animals only humans give names
which enable us to talk about others

people converse about others
wondering with whom to interact
trying to gauge what to expect

gossip itself becomes a game
of cooperation and defection
people may spread false information
to promote their own advantage

communication becomes crucial

if the group is so large that not
all interactions can be observed
then gossip replaces grooming

for efficient indirect reciprocity
in large groups language is needed

at the dawn of human evolution
it is likely that the social politics
of indirect reciprocity provided
the pivotal selection pressure
for the emergence of language

the winners of the games were
those who communicated well
who interpreted others clearly
who made themselves heard

he noted the fragrance of the roses
that was suspended in the night
what's in a name? he wondered

personally i prefer social norms
that classify proper cooperation
as good and defection as bad
these norms of indirect reciprocity
can be upheld if people combine
them with forgiveness

a balancing act confers stability here:
if i defect with a defector i incur a cost
that someone else might defect with me
but the cost is offset by the gain i had
of not paying the cost of cooperation
this cancelation makes the strategy stable

a Nash equilibrium?—a Nash equilibrium!

there is a formula which describes indirect
and direct reciprocity in a single framework

you love unification

i do

i grant the excitement of unification, she said
but is everything an analysis of cost and benefit?

we are in the world of natural selection
in that domain there is counting of payoffs
as well as reckoning of winners and losers
he said apologetically

but sometimes winners cooperate
he added hoping to impress her

this is not enough for me, she replied
my ambition is for more

but tell me of the remaining mechanisms

the third mechanism is kin selection
it can arise if individuals cooperate
with close genetic relatives but defect
with distant kin or unrelated individuals

if there is genetic encoding for cooperation
then this genetic material could be present
in both the donor and the recipient

natural selection can favor cooperation
between close relatives because the gene
for cooperation might have a direct gain

the approach suffers from acute problems
how the effect is analyzed and interpreted

the fourth mechanism is group selection
if there is competition between groups
then groups of cooperators could win

selection is operating on two levels
within groups selection favors defectors
between groups it favors cooperators

overall it could go one way or another
but cooperators could win in principle

it is also called multi-level selection
because the mechanism need not
be restricted to only two levels

there could be groups of groups
and groups of groups of groups
and so on... like Russian dolls

multi-level selection is useful
for the emergence of the first cell

a cell is a group of cooperating molecules
they compete within the cell for resources
but cells also compete with one another

then there can be aggregates of cells
that fight it out on a higher level

multi-level selection is relevant for humans
we form groups such as villages, towns,
countries, companies and those compete

competition between groups is problematic
it can lead to suffering and tragedy
it can induce hate against the out-group
it can be a source of malady, she shuddered

i realize it need not be that extreme
but in many cases it could be
hence the cooperation that is gained
within the group comes at a high price

i think it can also lead to cooperative
behavior that is questionable in itself:
cooperation in order to better attack
competing groups is very undesirable

she is unsatisfiable! he thought
which impressed him tremendously

the final mechanism is spatial selection
it can operate in physical or social space
where neighbors or friends help another

in structured populations cooperators
form clusters that can prevail and grow
even if surrounded by defectors

friends who are connected in a social network
may help one another and their cooperation
can expand and take over the population

this mechanism works even in absence
of strategic complexity or reciprocity

the mechanism has the potential to promote
the evolution of a basic cooperative instinct

whether this cooperative instinct evolves
depends on the structure of the population
and how individuals update their behavior

if they are introverted and only consider
what gives them the highest payoff now
then the mechanism does not work

if they are extroverted and willing to learn
from friends then cooperation can spread

winners are those whose friends cooperate
by being a cooperator you make it more likely
that your friends are cooperators too

i like this idea, she said

finally, he thought relieved

he was aware of the music again
recognizing the parodic andante amoroso
what a truly transcendent composer!

are you ready to pass judgment?

i am, she replied

Movement 2

after some reflection she said
i like all five mechanisms as tools
for explaining how cooperation
among biological organisms can
arise under natural selection

it is good that evolution can move beyond
competition as the only organizing force

cooperation as a principle of evolution
even as architect of biological complexity
is a step in the right direction

life is not only a brute struggle for survival
which is always won by selfish individuals

as selfishness is losing its grip
something greater moves into focus
we see cooperation everywhere

i like the idea that cooperation
is crucially involved in all moments
of great discovery in evolution
that it was present at the origin of life
that it gave rise to the first cell
to multi-cellularity, animal societies
and ultimately to human language

if the only force in evolution was
natural selection then it would be
surprising that in the human realm
we want people to be unselfish

i have particular interest in asking
which of the mechanisms contribute
decisively to human cooperation
which of them help us remove
the delusion of selfishness?
which of them pave the way
into a sustainable future?

humanity is at a turning point, a crossroad

we have reached the limits of the planet
so far our approach has been exploitative
destructive and irresponsible with respect
to the role of our stewardship of the earth

greed, selfishness, and ignorance
have distorted many human efforts

we need more cooperation on all levels
we urgently need global cooperation and
cooperation with future generations

for gaining sustainability we need willingness
to forgo some luxuries for the benefit of those
who will inherit this planet from us

let me explore how the five mechanisms
can help us to reach some of our goals

kin selection which augments cooperation
among close genetic relatives is useful
on small scales and within extended families
but does not solve the problem of how
to get cooperation on larger scales
it does not induce us to help strangers
or achieve global cooperation
the quest for true humanity is to move
beyond the confines of kin selection

we find a similar problem with group selection
it is useful for promoting cooperation between
individuals of the same group but the reverse
implication is that it hinders cooperation
between individuals from different groups

the in-group pro-sociality is accompanied
by an out-group anti-sociality which is concerning
we have witnessed that conflict between groups
fuels hatred, revenge, war, and even genocide

Movement 2

direct reciprocity works if our crucial
interactions are pairwise and repeated
it is a mechanism that leads to cooperation
among unrelated individuals and even
between members of different groups

many of our interactions are repeated
but not all fall into this category

clearly i want to see cooperation
in non-repeated fleeting encounters
without a shadow of the future

i want to see cooperation
with the poor, the hungry, the sick
and with those who are in prison
i demand cooperation with people
who are too weak to reciprocate

i acknowledge that direct reciprocity
leads to forgiveness and generosity
which are recommendable traits
but overall the emphasis is based
on what i call strategic selfishness

individuals are picking strategies
that maximize their own payoff
how can i be satisfied with that?

moreover should an individual use
unconditional cooperation then others
have an incentive to exploit her
how could that be acceptable to me?

i encourage unconditional cooperation
which i see not as submissive but confident

direct reciprocity is a preparation for
humans to go into the right direction
but it does not fully meet my demands

she paused

indirect reciprocity is an approach
that can work in large societies and
also for non-repeated interactions

what is required for this mechanism
to trigger widespread cooperation
is reliable information about our actions

an agreeable feature of the concept
is that generosity can be rewarded:
help and you shall receive help
give and you shall be given

i can also fathom that the mechanism
rewards a genuine cooperative attitude

if people are discerning of what truly
moves others to act in certain ways
then a social norm could incorporate
and reward what is true cooperation

it might lead to people who believe
that the world is a good place and
that cooperators will win in the end

a drawback of the mechanism
is the apparent need to withhold
cooperation from those who have
failed in some capacity in the past

but is it not our moral imperative
to welcome back into society
those people who have failed?

he wanted to insert something
but she said, bear with me

the social norm could distinguish
between those who truly make
an effort to return to cooperation
and those who are continuing
on the road of defection

in anticipation we can reward the former
but withhold cooperation from the latter

is this what you wanted to say?

probably... do you read my mind?

you are an open book, she thought

here is the problem, she continued
withholding cooperation or ostracism
is a kind of punishment but alas
i prefer to go without punishment
i dislike any form of punishment

if God is present in every person
how can you find a justification
for the punishment of a person?
even for withholding cooperation?

instead the better approach must
be to appeal to the goodness that
is innermost essence of everyone
do you follow me there?

i follow you but the question is
how can this goal be achieved?

the answer to your question
leads us to the fifth mechanism
which you call spatial selection

here a cooperative instinct
without strategic selfishness
without retaliation can spread
—under certain conditions

some structures are more conducive
than others and in one approach
it was found that an ideal society
contains strong pairwise relationships

cooperation can proliferate
if people learn from others
if people attempt to imitate
the cooperative disposition
of those that are already
surrounded by cooperators

you do well if your friends cooperate
your friends are more likely to cooperate
if they see that you are a cooperator

this property should be to my liking
you achieve cooperation among humans
if you lead by example

if the central nodes in a society
become beacons for cooperation
there is hope that others will follow
and become cooperative too

imagine a society where cooperators
are strategically placed into the center

after some contemplation she said
we need to move entirely beyond
the myopic confines of selfishness

a true supercooperator is one
who does not consider her payoff
but the combined payoff of others

that would make her a saint, he said

and this is our calling, she affirmed

the music had just ebbed away
they were suddenly alone again
enveloped by the summer night
by roses and busts in attendance

how would you compare the treasures
that are offered by different religions?

o my good teacher, i have seen so little
sparse beyond imagination is my knowledge
however you choose to think about me

all religions offer valuable ways to God
there is not one i elevate above others
in my Father's house are many mansions

God loves his children uniformly
not one is preferred in the eyes of the Lord

each one appears different at the surface
providing diverse council and illumination
but all come to the same truth in depth

religion is a passage through exile
our best friend on the journey of life

every single road that is traveled
by a sincere loving heart leads to God

there are as many ways to God
as there are children of God

each person, my good teacher
has her own way toward God
be a light unto yourself!

some ways lead through deserts
others over mountain ranges
some people need to swim
from one island to the next
others walk on sheets of glass
suspended above the world

each way must respect others
no way can obstruct another
they are all meant to unfold
in parallel toward one goal

life is not the easiest for the soul
but the most meaningful

when he said there is no way to the Father
other than through me he implied twofold

first there is no way to God
other than through God

second the sacrifice he was about to bring
assured salvation for all people

God is the way, the truth, and the life

they had reached a clearing in the forest
which opened to an ancient monastery

they saw people gathering in the church
whose outfits differed markedly from theirs
the priests were tall black hooded figures
the women wore bright head scarfs

one priest held up the book, the logos
and people stepped forward to kiss it

her heart poured out to them

can we join them? she asked the teacher

let us see if they invite us, he answered

waiting there she thought: if you love God
you see beautiful mystery everywhere
you realize how amazing this world is
everything becomes infinitely meaningful
because God gives meaning

MOVEMENT 3

1

they explored corridors leading away
from the courtyard of the university

can everyone study here? she asked
knowledge is a public good, he replied

does a university teach her students
knowledge or wisdom? does she show
them how to solve technical problems
or tutor them how to deal with life?

life is the university, he answered

the university has buildings
but those are not the university
the university has lecture halls
but those are not the university

instead it is carried forward
in the minds of its students
the students are the teachers
the teachers are the students

thirst for learning can never be stilled
we must know and we will know

learning prepares the soil
but life brings us the seeds
which germinate into flowers
that delight the heavens

a proper university is a paradise on earth
a garden of Eden prepared for us by God
that we may strive under the branches
of the ominous tree of knowledge

the students are the teachers? she asked

grey my dear friend is all theory
but green is the golden tree of life

what have you consumed?

poetry, he answered, discrete infinity!

the knowledge that replicates
in the petri dishes of the university
gives rise to creative conjectures
and to celebrated conclusions

all is derivative of one trait...

language cross-linked our minds
it gave bipedal apes access
to a universe of knowledge

language enabled primates
to leave the shelter of the forest
to migrate through the savanna
into the arms of the university

i feel so exhilarated in these walls
the smell has not changed at all
for me this is the drug that stays

i love the dust of scholarship
especially as a fleeting visitor
an unchained spirit, a shadow

calm down! she pleaded

language is difficult to grasp
all else is easy in comparison
he went on in excitement

suddenly an image of a famous
painting drew their attention

on a wall an announcement of
an academic event in linguistics
used Brueghel's Tower of Babel
to catch prospective listeners

this painting we could have seen
in the museum for sure, he said

we have missed it, she agreed

first was the library of Babel
then the museum of Babel
and now the tower of Babel
are we in the university of Babel?

what would that be?

the place that contains all classes
that are combinatorically possible

does language brings us to God?
she wondered

it elevates us over mere genetics
it facilitates a new mode of evolution
it makes infinite use of finite media
it is a tower that reaches the heavens

while this one failed language succeeded

she looked at him

moreover, he said, there is a mathematical
approach to language because nothing is
beyond the reach of mathematics

nothing? she smiled

nothing at all, he confirmed

we begin with an alphabet
which is a set of symbols
we can use the binary alphabet
which has two symbols 0 and 1
or we can use a larger alphabet
for example the letters of English

to proceed with simplicity
but without loss of generality
we use the binary alphabet
to make "sentences"

next to the Tower of Babel was a blackboard
how convenient! it was a university after all!
there was a sign that said "do not erase"
despite the injunction the slate was blank

our alphabet is the set 0 and 1

she took the chalk and wrote {0, 1}

now imagine all sentences that
can be written with this alphabet
these are all the binary sequences

she wrote 0,1,00,01,10,11,000,...

there are infinitely many sentences
as many as integers

i cannot write all of them, she said

for sure

a language is a set of sentences
a sentence belongs to the set or not

write a language that has three sentences

she wrote {01,110,1000}

a finite language has finitely many sentences
while an infinite language has infinitely many

there are infinitely many finite languages
—as many as integers
there are infinitely many infinite languages
—as many as real numbers

integers are countable, reals are uncountable
there are many more reals than integers

human languages are infinite: no finite
list can contain all sentences of English

here is an example of an infinite language
{0,01,011,0111,...} each sentence starts
with 0 followed by a sequence of 1s

another example of an infinite language is
{01,0011,000111,...} each sentence contains
a sequence of 0s followed by a sequence of 1s
but both sequences have the same length

next we ask: what is a grammar?
a grammar is a finite list of rewrite rules
which defines a language

for the first language we write
S → 0A
A → 1A
A → nothing

S denotes "sentence," A is a place holder
0 and 1 are elements of the alphabet
the arrow means "can be rewritten as"

sentence S can be rewritten as 0A
A can be rewritten as 1A
A can be rewritten as "nothing"

once the last rule is used the sentence is done
if all place holders are gone a sentence is finished

we can use the grammar to generate
S → 0A → 01A → 011A → 011

the grammar accepts the sentence 011

do you accept this?

i do, she replied

it is easy to see that the grammar
does not accept the sentence 0101
this sentence is ungrammatical
it does not belong to that language

for the second language we write
S → 0S1
S → nothing

we can use this grammar to generate
S → 0S1 → 00S11 → 000S111 → 000111

therefore 000111 is grammatical here
in contrast 011 would be ungrammatical

imagine 25 place holders and 99 rules
the question if a sentence is accepted
by that grammar could be hard to answer

in fact many problems in mathematics
can be formulated as: does a particular
grammar accept a certain sentence?

a mathematical theorem is a sentence
a proof is the derivation of the sentence
using the rewrite rules of the grammar
which are the axioms of that field

the question if two distinct grammars accept
the same language is in general undecidable

the mathematical approach to language
and grammar is not only at the foundation
of mathematics but also of computer science

a grammar is equivalent to a digital computer
language is the world of discrete infinity
and the same is true of digital machines

a simple machine is a finite state automaton
it has a finite number of states
when jumping from one state to another
it emits a symbol of the alphabet

you feed the machine an input sentence
that is a binary sequence and then you
check if the machine accepts that sequence

our first example is a finite state grammar
for each finite state grammar there is a
finite state automaton that does the job

Movement 3

the second example belongs to the more
general class of context-free grammars

the corresponding machines are
finite-state automata with a memory stack
they can access the top register in their stack
moving the other registers up or down
they are more powerful than finite-state automata

no finite-state automaton accepts the language
of our second example since the sequences of
0s and 1s must have the same length but can
be arbitrarily long

on top of the hierarchy are Turing machines
they are finite-state automata with a tape
in each position of the tape is written 0 or 1
a read/write head is moving over the tape
the head itself is a finite-state automaton
the tape serves as memory, it is unbounded

a Turing machine is equivalent to a grammar
with unrestricted rewrite rules: any string of
place holders and elements of the alphabet
can be rewritten as another string

the set of all Turing machines accepts
those languages that have a grammar
they are called semi-decidable languages

they have two subsets: recursively
enumerable and co-recursively enumerable

this is quite some jargon, she said

please forgive me, i will explain

for each grammar there is a Turing machine
that accepts the corresponding language
the machine receives as input a sentence
and computes if it belongs to the language

there are three possibilities

first: for each input the machine stops and
announces if the sentence belongs or not
such a language is called "decidable"

second: for each input which belongs
the machine stops after some time
and announces this positive result
but if a sentence does not belong
the machine may compute forever

in this case the language is called
"recursively enumerable"
we can list sentences that belong

third: for each input which does not belong
the machine stops after some time
and announces this negative result
but if a sentence does belong
the machine may compute forever

this type of language is called
"co-recursively enumerable"
we can list sentences that do not belong

the union of the sets recursively enumerable and
co-recursively enumerable is called semi-decidable
the intersection of the two sets is called decidable

she drew the two sets on the blackboard
labeled them, their union, and their intersection

all problems that mathematicians solve
are in the class of decidable languages
if they were to select random problems
from the vast universe of all problems
most all of them would be undecidable

let me summarize, she said slightly vexed
nothing is beyond the reach of mathematics
fine! but if most problems in mathematics are
undecidable what is the good of mathematics?

let us not go there for now, he pleaded
let us do that another time on another tape

Movement 3 191

after some reflection he said
much can be done with decidable problems
worlds can be staked out and illuminated

there was a celebrated mathematician
who gave yearly strawberry parties
he mailed printed invitation cards
on each card he filled in the name
of the person and then checked either
"you are invited" or "you are not invited"

in this way he attempted to reduce
a semi-decidable to a decidable problem

a grammar is a finite list of rewrite rules
there are as many grammars as integers
for each grammar there is a Turing machine
for each Turing machine there is a grammar
Turing machines are as numerous as integers
hence they can be indexed by integers

i can give you an example for a language
that is semi-decidable but not decidable

i am curious, she said

let M be the integer index of a Turing machine
let w denote the input that is presented

the desired language contains all pairs *(M,w)*
such that machine M halts on input w

what a strange language! she exclaimed

to study this language you need a Turing
machine that simulates all Turing machines
this is called a universal Turing machine

the machine checks pairs *(M,w)*
after a few steps of computation on a pair
it starts to evaluate a new pair
pairs that halt will be done after some time
and the machine can list them but for other
pairs the computation goes on forever

therefore the language is semi-decidable
but not decidable, it is recursively enumerable

is this example revealing? she wondered

it reminds me of a story where an angel says
to a philosopher: you can ask God a question
the philosopher sees an amazing opportunity
after long reflection he says my question is:
what is the pair of the best possible questions
that i could ask and its answer?

the angel goes to God who computes quickly
the angel returns and says: the best question
you could have asked is the question you did
ask and the answer is the one i just gave you

she smiled but seemed lost in thoughts
they sat down on a bench in a lecture room

let us now think about language acquisition
how does a child learn language? he said

the child receives sentences of the language
after some time it generates sentences

in order to do this the child has acquired
an internal representation of the grammar

the child is not told grammatical rules
instead the rules have to be inferred
from the sentences that are provided

learning grammar from example sentences
is called learning by inductive inference

the problem is: any finite list of sentences
is compatible with infinitely many grammars

a mathematical theorem states:
the process can only succeed if the learner
uses a restricted search space of grammars

there are different versions of this theorem
depending on the details of the process
but all point to the same conclusion:
success requires the learner to be restricted

blank slate learning is not possible
the learner needs a restricted search space

now a set of languages is learnable
if each language in the set is learnable

in the context of natural language acquisition
the theory for the restricted search space used
by the human brain is called universal grammar

amusingly since universal grammar is a theory
of a set of grammars it is not a grammar itself

as evolution induced variation in brain structure
our ancestors used different universal grammars

hence universal grammar is neither a grammar
nor universal—the name comes from Chomsky's
intent to find grammatical elements that are
shared by all 6000 human languages

since we are talking about human languages
she said, their productions are more
than just sequences of zeros and ones
does the mathematical approach really
capture what human language is about?

so far we have mostly discussed syntax
but there are also phonetics and semantics

syntax deals with sentence structure
and if sentences are grammatical or not

phonetics describes sound production
and perception—it is the interface
between the language machinery
and the auditory and vocal organs

semantics has to do with meaning
it is the interface of language and the world

semantics leads to philosophical questions
what is the meaning of a word?
where does meaning come from?

bringing us back to Plato, she said

or forward to Wittgenstein, he said
whose aim was to end philosophy
he wanted to be the last philosopher!
some say his first attempt failed
but his second attempt succeeded!

fiction! she exclaimed
anybody can still pose as a philosopher

certainly in a cafe, he replied

in a broader sense syntax is anything rule-based
it can include rules of phonetics and semantics

we extend the formal approach to add semantics
by considering sentence-meaning pairs

a language becomes a matrix of such pairs
some are in the language, others are not
the grammar generates that matrix
we are still in the world of discrete infinity

where do the meanings come from?

they are in the restricted search space
they specify how we parse the world
they emanate from the underlying reality
they derive from the world of forms

and we remember them?

we have them in us

they can be selected by the data
but data do not generate them
there must be prior constraints
before any of the data arrive
this is a mathematical necessity

universal grammar in a broader sense
contains meanings that are labeled
by linguistic forms, he continued

a universal grammar of semantics
becomes a logical necessity

every organism that infers rules from examples
has a universal grammar of a kind

the search space for the learning task is given
by genetics, by the developmental process
by the laws of nature and of mathematics

you can say it is given by God

any generalization from examples
requires a restricted search space

i find this immensely fascinating:
inductive inference occurs not only in
language acquisition but in any learning
process where you try to make sense
of some examples or some data

the scientist uses inductive inference
when trying to formulate laws of nature
the process of science cannot succeed
if scientists were entirely open-minded
the process must start with a restricted
search space and can never go beyond it

the restriction can be understood
as a universal grammar of science

therefore human science is not
an objective description of reality
instead it arises at the interface
of the human brain and nature

the scientific quest works out
if the grammar used by nature
is in our search space, she said

precisely! and a benevolent creator
would certainly arrange it like this

did you mention a cafe? she asked

2

she got up early as was her custom
during morning prayers in the chapel
she was shivering under her hood
each day is God's gift, she thought

later when working in the garden
she was thinking of sowing salt
but she had neither donkey nor ox
she reflected on the futility of time

then one of the milkmaids came
and revealed visitors were here
who had asked to speak to her
visitors to see me? she replied

she was both surprised and not
both knowing and unknowing
in all those years in the village
no one had come to see her

she touched the earth once more
inhaled the fragrance of the soil
she wondered, what gives me the
right to choose my own path?

if i do not choose my path
who chooses for me?
if i choose my path
who does the choosing?

she got up washed her hands
in the fountain's cold water
she paused and drank from it
oh how she loved the taste!

she thought of mountain streams
that carried the ice cold water
of the blue glaciers high above
into the deep lake in the valley

in summer swimming in the lake
diving in its serene effulgence
among quivering schools of fish
her eyes touching living water

she knew that the cells of her body
were carrying within the primordial
ocean of truth and of life's origination

is knowledge memory or premonition
mixed in the turbulences of time
with eons beginning yet unending?

when she entered the room
she saw two men standing there
they bowed to her respectfully

she wondered if their respect
was meant for someone else
but beside her was no second
who had entered the room

she bowed more deeply in return
because signaling the superiority
of the other was her custom

their clothes were finer than
those of people in the village
finer than those of the clergy
in the rural churches around

she thought those men who
are not from here must hold
high office in a distant place

thank you, madam, for granting
us this audience, one of them
began with a courtly politeness

we are visitors to this beautiful
spot of the world because it is
our duteous obligation to convey
a certain message of significance

Movement 3

if you are coming from afar
and your message is important
you may have found the wrong place
she replied, this is a simple village

forgive us, madam, but we are
firmly assured that we have
reached the correct destination

my lords, if your message is
of relevance then certainly
it cannot be intended for me
the prior of the abbey yonder
would be a proper recipient

madam, our word is for you

my lords, it is possible that
you mistake me for another
i am a worker and a maid
i am a servant of the poor
and only a helper of helpers

madam, we are confident
beyond any doubt that we
are facing the right person

and yet—forgive me, my lords—
i cannot deem myself to be the
recipient of important messages

then she was silent while the
images of her morning returned
why do they call me "madam"?
no one has addressed me like this

with her eyes lowered she asked
what if i preferred to remain
ignorant of your intelligence?

we venture to say, madam, even
without explicit words you will
discover the facts in your heart
maybe not today but tomorrow

they held a regardful silence

it is furthermore our conviction
that you do not reject anyone
who applies to you in earnest
you have not done this before

again after a polite intermission
are we correct in assuming that
your teacher has prepared you
for this particular moment?

my good teacher has prepared
me for many moments

would you be so kind to give us
your precious time and permit us
to relate our mission in detail?

my time is not prized, she said
i have unlimited abundance of it
in every single day

your time is of inestimable value
for those who have your attention
he said bowing as if accepting a gift

we would like to present for your
kind consideration some materials
which we have brought with us

she sat down

after a moment of hesitation which
she noticed but did not understand
they followed her lead and sat down

they were facing her across the table
they placed several bound folders
on its heavy but worn oaken surface

there is a distinct office of service
which has been vacant for years
people are hoping it will be filled
when the right opportunity arises

for decades there has been intense
searching for a suitable candidate

the august office is not inherited
neither money nor influence can gain it
it is unreachable for all who desire it

the wise know in their heart
that they cannot fulfill the objective
which the office demands

the unwise apply but the search
does not linger with them

the procedure is incorruptible
it ignores status and high birth
it discredits power and wealth
it looks into the hearts of people

according to legends of old
in every age there is at most
one befitting candidate
one entirely pure heart

unbending realists would add
one incarnation of the form

having searched all corners of
the earth our emissaries returned
empty handed year after year

at one time a message arrived
from this place that an image
of the goddess of wisdom
had impressed and exhausted
the knowledge of her teachers
and that more advanced tutors
had been urgently requested

by unfathomable chance
this message received regard
in some chambers of the search
this was many years ago

your good teacher was sent here
he is—a thousand apologies if this
comes as surprise for you—one
of our trusted agents of search

the astonishment on her face
made him now pause...

...i guess it must be a surprise
please accept our humble regret
the clockwork of the search is intricate
and sometimes reaches too deep

at first his reports received little
notice but gradually they moved
upward to higher echelons

in recent years in fruition of time
we read his accounts with eagerness
we studied the evidence he sent us
the wisest of the wise searched the
scriptures of old and used all the
science of new to learn about you

we relied not on his material alone
but diligently sent other emissaries
these were people who passed by
wandering teachers, monks, aides

sometimes they were poor souls
to whom you showed kindness or
sick people for whom you cared

he paused and looked at the
other man who said

the beggar to whom you gave
your cloak—your only cloak—
was genuine but the coincidental
observer in that particular season
of lent was one of our agents

indirect reciprocity! she thought
flowing upstream or downstream
through the veins of humanity

all the information was carefully
evaluated, the man continued
our process is slow and does not
jump to premature conclusions

our deliberations are accompanied
by prayer and deep meditation
we trust our intentions are pure

there are also agents at work charged
with finding evidence to the contrary
they have to search especially hard
they often prove unmistakably that
a conjectured candidate is unsuitable

here these *advocati diaboli*—to use
an ancient term—found nothing
they became your fervent supporters

he talked with prudent consideration
making pauses to gauge her reaction
he frequently looked at the other man
for reassurance and confirmation

her penetrating eyes were on his
and sometimes on the other man's
who was observing her intently
both were firmly holding her gaze

suddenly she was aware that
people rarely held her glance
not even her esteemed teacher
Lina had been the exception

in short, madam, after many years
of careful and rigorous investigation
our search is concluded

he waited for her response which
came after a few moments as

i am well pleased that your
meticulous work finds fruition
may your efforts be noble
your path be blessed by God

all were silent for some time
it seemed as if the conversation
had reached a certain impasse

then the man resumed
we have reason to believe...

the other man made a gesture
which made him stop and restart

we have been sent here entrusted
with the holy mission to inform you
that you are the target of the search

you are the choice of the order
the choice of the committee
the choice of the people
even the choice of God
as far as we can discern

you are the form the search specifies
the input that halts the machine

she looked at them

we further announce the conjecture
that your identity is revealed to us
that yours is a great saintly soul
which has matured over many lives

you are a bodhisattva of compassion
an avatar of Lakshmi, of Saraswati
you are Radha, Meera, Sujata
you led Aeneas out of the burning Troy

you are an incarnation that comes
in every age usually appearing as
an orphan often adopting the role
of a servant by your own choice

you claim nothing for yourself
you are unconfused by selfishness
you resist passion and desire
all you have you share with others
your life is fully devoted to God

it is our solemn hope
that you will accept our suit
the petition of the realm

she got up with resolution
and walked to the window
they rose at once as she did
but remained near the table

she looked out of the window
she noticed the people at work
she saw tasks where she could
have been of help right now

she wanted to be among them
she saw her garden in the distance
the gentle hill behind the village
the path leading up to the top

oh how she longed to be there
screening the surface of the
ocean for plain simple truth

she saw children at play

she looked up at the clouds
wondering if there would be rain
which would refresh the fields,
the animals, the gardens

then she turned around
and addressed them thus

this world is my world
there is no other world for me
here i came as an orphan
these villagers took me in
they fed me when i was hungry
they nourished me when i was weary
i am devoted to them
i love them dearly

no malice grows among them
i help wherever i am able
it is my call to serve them
in simple unimpressive ways

there are sick people here
who wait for me every evening
there are mourners who need comfort
there are broken hearts searching for hope
there are families who rely on me
to ease their hardship

here i am rooted, here i am working
here i am striving, here i will die

this is my one and only call
this is my one and only...

she wanted to say "love"
but did not finish the sentence
she looked out of the window

had they declared her void of passion?
empty of desire? how wrong they were!

her thoughts wandered... there are those
beautiful conversations with the teacher
they transport me to worlds beyond...
beyond this village, beyond those hills

is there a world beyond? is this what
he wanted me to see all those years?
the world beyond? the science of love?
the book of nature?... she fell silent

then she turned to them again

i do not know, my lords
what has moved you to make
such grand remarks about me
but the information you reveal
is not inside me, i cannot find it

moreover let me remind you
that nobody is good before God
nobody stands without sin
before the Lord of the world

whatever it is that your dignified
office demands it is not for me
to possess the wanted distinction

it was quiet in the room

both men had lowered their eyes
they tried to pick up the line of hope
that had glided to the floor

my lady, you came here long ago
you have transformed this village
you may not have noticed it yet
but one day you will see clearly
this village is unlike any other

a blessing came over this place
many years ago when a young
orphan stood in front of a door
which had no handle outside
which was opened for her

why did he know the image?

the door is the entrance to the
human soul, the divine stands
in front of the dwelling but the
gate must be opened from within

this door was opened for you
you entered and blessed them
you dined and lived with them
and everything was changed

i am not the divine, she protested

the good which acts in every
person which moves the soul
and illuminates the mind and
disperses the somber clouds
of selfishness is from God

the good works in subtle ways
it is a very gentle light
it can only be perceived
by those searching for it
by those who open the door
to let the light fall inside
and allow you to enter

only God is good, she insisted

most certainly, madam, it is true
that the goodness of God is of a
different kind as the philosopher
himself has taught us long ago

God is the source of all goodness
all else receives goodness from God

has the philosopher taught you?
she wondered

however you choose to call it
my lady, it spreads from you
to others and such a treasure
implies an obligation, a duty

you have transformed this village
there is no acrimony here anymore
as you have formulated it yourself
now the world wants to be healed!

the world has opened its door
it is a large and magnificent door
it is almost always firmly closed
but now in this moment of history
in this one realm it is wide open

now that you are standing in front
of this door which was specifically
opened for you, can you pass by?
can you nullify the hopes of many?

she was silent

be reassured we do not declare
you void of all passion of all desire
while there is no selfishness within you
the love for the Lord consumes you
we know this: your desire is for God
your life's passion is to glorify Him

he had not failed to impress her
and a prolonged silence ensued

as we have noted you are a
bodhisattva of compassion
your fine soul has matured
over a multitude of lives
it was this property which has
commended you in the search

and yet such knowledge is not
within me, she repeated

my lady, we think there are more
memories than you can fathom
we may be able to help you find
some of those nearly forgotten
images, moments, preferences

the information we have assembled
has persuaded us and everyone
who has participated in the search
it might also convince you in the end
please consider it with open heart

we have done our work with diligence
here is a summary of what we found
over the decade and even longer

he opened one of the folders

here is a poem of Enheduanna
no copy existed in our libraries
it was hard for us to secure it

in comparison a homework of yours
from long ago even from the time
before your teacher arrived here

we analyzed the flow, the rhythm
the current, the choice of words
the stream of consciousness

in two distinct languages... she said

there is only one universal grammar
of love and of truth, he countered

here are some poems by Meera
revealing her passion for God

here is a map of Troy showing
the secret passage known to you

then he reached into a bag
which she had not noticed before

here is the flute he played for you
and that he stopped playing
when the two of you were separated

she startled... a flute... separated?

Movement 3

you are in my eyes
you are in my mind
you are in my thoughts

then where am i not?

in my fate

she took the flute
her fingers trembled

this is not...

it cannot be...

this is not the original?

it is a replica, the man replied
carefully crafted after the original

and the original?

in possession of the order
a priceless possession
but not in good condition

playable?

i do not think so

he never wanted it to be played
by anyone else... please know this!
are you sure you have the original?

he presented another musical device
and placed it in her hands

do you know what instrument
this one here is? he asked

a veena, she answered at once

do you know how to play it?

she moved her fingers

i do know how to play it, she replied
but i don't know why...

she seemed lost in thoughts
as if entering a trance-like state

it is not common in our realm
he explained

i wish to reintroduce it, she said
coming back from a dream

she walked toward the table
she leaned over the folder
which contained many papers
some printed others handwritten
there were drawings and maps

she began reading with devotion
around her the room disappeared

the men withdrew from the table
at times she called them back
to ask about a certain document

hours passed

she opened the second folder

she realized these folders were
only summaries, excerpts, first
glimpses of a larger body of work

they were entrances to a vast library
which contained innumerable books

they brought her a glass of water
she thanked them profusely

then another one and again

they offered her tea but she declined

i am so sorry i am keeping you
she said at some point

Movement 3

madam, it is our sacred duty

the sun was near setting
but she did not notice

...Fujiwara Akiko, wife of the emperor Ichijo
mother of two emperors Go-Ichijo and Go-Suzaku

Fujiwara Kaoruko, her lady waiting
author of *The Tale of Genji*
retired with the Empress Shoshi
to the shores of Lake Biwa...

...in that lake is an island with a temple
devoted to one whose name means
"she who possesses purifying speech,
pooling waters, ponds, and lakes"

healing powers of living waters

waters that purify
speech that purifies
knowledge that purifies

she who brings forth art, music, dance,
language, literature, poetry, philosophy,
and all creative work whose flow through
time accompanies the stream of life

she who reminds the pilgrim
to meditate on virtue and on
the meaning of one's choices,
actions, and trajectories

she, white as the moon
holding a book and a pen
adorned by pearls or leaves
carrying a vessel of water

the pearls reflecting the power of meditation
are innermost likenesses of selflessness

accompanied by a swan who if offered a mixture
of milk and water can drink the milk alone
discriminating between essence and appearance
eternal and transient, form and manifestation

she composes on a veena representing creative
arts and sciences, knowledge, and harmony

imaginary travel companion to a renowned
Tibetan monk who crafted poems for her

with every page she sunk deeper
into a state of recalling memories
that existed in time immemorial
or that will reoccur in a far future

the membrane between form
and knowledge thereof was lifted
the two concepts fused into one
the highest kind of knowledge
is intuition of the Form Herself

she knew it now

after sieving through eternity
she rose from the table and
walked toward the window
now it was dark outside

facing the window helped her to hide
what was to come—she started to cry

she did not know why

she rarely cried except when mourning Lina
but now the reason was different
when the call arrives
when you realize who you are
when you feel God's presence within
the emotions give way
the tears are the baptism of a new person

Movement 3

the old shell is filled with new understanding
this is my beloved child which i have chosen
this is who i am, this is my inner self

she wept quietly—her body shook

the men were embarrassed
they did not know what to do
they pretended not to notice

after some time she composed herself
but kept looking out of the window

finally one of the men said
madam, we wish to add that you
alone are the judge of our work
our conjecture can only be true
if you find resonance inside you
if you detect none then one word
from you will silence our suit forever

she nodded

her loving heart opened to their quest
which was noble and blessed by God

she turned to them

my lords, there is no doubt that
the materials you have presented
evoke in me responses which are
vague and elusive yet strong and
overwhelming, even indescribable

how strange it must seem
but i am undeniably connected
to the fates of people and
to events that are hinted at
in your vast collection

there are memories within me
coming from inexplicable sources

as soon as she had admitted
this realization something in
the fabric of the instantiated
universe had fallen into place

some threads were connecting
some numbers found a match
some harmonies resonated

at that moment the pendulum
on the mantelpiece stopped
all three of them noticed it
although neither had been
aware of the clock before

what an elegant wooden
time piece in this village
one of the men contemplated

you notice time when she halts
was her reflection—time stood still

in this case which was the solemn hope
of our heart we are honored to repeat
the dispatch that was entrusted to us

madam, we inform you that you are
the choice of the innermost core
which governs this realm

it is our sacred duty to convey
to you the following question:
in the name of the committee
in the name of the government
in the name of the people you love
do you accept to serve and
to extend the unbroken line?

however vague that formulation was
she understood the implied meaning

my noble lords, i trust you will grant
me some fleeting moment to consider
a question of such relevance

Movement 3

madam, we give you any time
you consider appropriate

i only request a single night
i expect you to return tomorrow
and then you are at liberty
to renew your application

we are at your disposal, madam

i wish you a blessed night, my lords

they bowed to her and she to them

3

i love this place
it is almost midnight
but the small cafe here is still open
it is a late night institution
it has only a few tables

is it always open?

they close eventually
but maybe not this night

what is it about this night?

we can sit outside by the fountain

what is your summary so far?

my summary? she asked

what do you conclude?

is it for me to conclude or for you?

for both of us, he replied

that's fair

to reach a conclusion about everything...

...about everything?—everything!

we must examine the question...

...what is mathematics?

how did you know? he asked

oh it is so obvious
it is midnight
it is midsummer night midnight
it is a magic night
the night of all nights
you are with me
what else could be on your mind
other than mathematics?

Movement 3

let us order some coffee, he said

we will be up all night

we will anyway

so what is mathematics?

when we do mathematics
we search for fundamental truth
about numbers, sets, shapes

we can ask many questions
for some we receive answers

how many prime numbers are there?
the answer is: infinitely many

how many prime pairs are there?
these are primes separated by 2
such as 3 and 5 or 29 and 31

what is the answer to this question?

the answer is not known yet
the conjecture is infinitely many
but nobody has proven it

whatever the answer will be
it does not depend on us
we are not making it up
we are discovering it
the answer is... out there

out where?

that is precisely the point!

how many Platonic solids are there?
the faces of a Platonic solid are regular
structures identical in shape and size
in three dimensions there are five
in four dimensions there are six
in all higher dimensions there are three

the coffee arrived in three dimensions
on a metal tray with a glass of water

the coffee in this city is considered...

but the way she looked at him
made it clear he did not need
to continue that particular line
of culinary reasoning prompted
by his infatuation with a place

he attempted to recover ground with:
someone said to be successful in this city
it is not enough to have no ideas
you must also be unable to realize them

Mahler remarked if the world ends
he would move here because in this city
everything happens fifty years later

she laughed

the city was always loved by many
but did she ever love in return?

more people died here, they say
than were born here

but back to mathematics
which is neither born nor dies

for a circle what is the ratio
of circumference to diameter?
the answer is the well known
universally beloved number pi

does she love in return? she asked

she loves to show up everywhere

the value of pi is given to us—but how?
who or what gifts this number to us?

we know that pi is an irrational number
it is not the fraction of any two integers
the digits of pi never end and they never
settle into a permanently repeating pattern

pi is also a transcendental number
it is not the solution of any polynomial
that has rational coefficients

this feature implies that the ancient quest
of squaring the circle using a compass
and a straightedge cannot be achieved

Archimedes discovered an algorithm
that enabled him to calculate pi
but the first exact formula was found
by the indian mathematician Madhava

pi is believed to be a normal number
which is defined by the property that
no sequence is favored over any other

what a beautiful property! she said

it can be shown that almost
all real numbers are normal
being normal is very normal

even better! she said joyfully
then beauty is ubiquitous

but very few specific numbers
have been proven to be normal
pi is only conjectured to be normal

here is another suitable fact
for a midsummer night's dream:
in contrast to our celebrated pi
the number for the probability
that a random program halts
can be proven to be normal
but it is non-computable

you can't have it all, she lamented

he looked at her

after some reflection she said
if we use a code to turn letters
into numbers then every book
becomes one long number

if a normal number contains
every sequence of any length
then it contains every book

yes this is true, he said

the fabric of mathematics contains
a representation of everything
of every event, every narrative
every poem, every Platonic form

they were silent

the digits of pi, the prime numbers
are not caused by forces of nature
they do not arise from physics
they are not products of evolution
they are neither born nor do they die
they are not in time, they just are

they are in an underlying timeless reality
which we experience but do not invent

then we can conclude there is
such an underlying reality?

i think we can

she was reflective looking over the
small place and its nightly visitors
two waiters served the tables of
the cafe which were outside

most people were in conversations
some intense others cheerful
what were their topics?

Movement 3

imagine a book that lists all ongoing
conversations of people in a city
the book can be found among
the digits of any normal number

statements about mathematics
are in the realm of metamathematics

metamathematics in a midsummer
night's dream, he suddenly thought

metamathematics? she wondered

"2 + 2 = 4" is mathematics
"2 + 2 = 4 is true" is metamathematics
the term was coined by David Hilbert
who was a preeminent mathematician

John von Neumann who invented game
theory, automata theory, who built the
first programmable computer and so on
considered himself a failure because he
thought he was only third best of his time

whom did he rank above himself?

first Hilbert and second the man
with the decidable strawberry party

it all comes together, she remarked

the four main schools concerning
the foundations of mathematics are
mathematical platonism, formalism,
intuitionism, and logicism

mathematical platonism is the view that
mathematical objects exist independently
of human activities and of all processes
that occur in the material universe

formalism on the other hand holds that
mathematics is a game whose rules
stipulate how to manipulate sequences

formalism has no particular commitment
to the existence of mathematical objects
no commitment to meaning or ontology
the game could be about... nothing

but formalism still admits the possibility
of interpreting the transformations

the interpretation is semantics
while the formalism is syntax
truth resides within syntax
and does not require semantics

formalism was advanced by Hilbert
but he was a realist since he believed
there is only one true mathematics
for him mathematics is a game but not
an arbitrary one: mathematics is real

if we adopt this position we are back
in the realm of mathematical platonism

intuitionism is the view that mathematics
is a mental construct of humans
it is the use of clear consistent methods
but not the discovery of principles
that exist in an objective reality

intuitionism is a denial of platonism
and again i do not see how that view
could be useful or even self-consistent

finally logicism is the perspective that
mathematics is an extension of logic
the aim is to derive all statements
of mathematics from symbolic logic

logicism is not a denial of platonism
but redefines the fundamental objects

mathematical platonism is sometimes
challenged for the following problem:

if the mathematical objects exist
independently of any human activity
how can we know about them?

they got distracted by a waiter
bringing them more water

this water comes from the mountains...

what here is not amazing? she asked

what here is not to love? he thought

a mathematician's activity is suggestive
of the existence of an underlying reality
each day she probes underlying reality
hoping to grasp some of its properties

i knew a mathematician who would miss lunch
if he had discovered something in the morning
whenever i saw him at lunch which was almost
every day i was sad for him and for mathematics

she leaned forward

do you see the chess players over there?

i have noticed them

is chess an invention or a discovery?

one could say chess is a human invention
the people who came up with the game
picked certain rules which were modified
over time to make it more interesting
the queen became more powerful

how thoughtful! she remarked

the rules were selected to be suitable
for preferences of the human mind
nevertheless chess and all other
such games are platonic objects

if you focus on a specific game
you can ask questions about it
answers to those questions will
come from the underlying reality
they do not depend on matter
not on physics not on biology

can you force mate with two knights?
is a rook versus bishop endgame won?
for a given position is there a winning
line for white? or for black? or a draw?

the answers are properties
of the platonic object itself

the rules of the chess game as it
is played by people have changed
over time but each version of
the game is a platonic object
with unchanging properties

do you mean each version of chess
is picked from the world of forms?

yes exactly!

the underlying reality contains
every version of chess and other
games that could be of interest?

yes it has an infinite library of games

is underlying reality like the library of Babel?

it contains that library and many others

remember we concluded the library of Babel
was small—only finite—while the underlying
reality contains every finite and infinite library
though hopefully not in physical manifestation

that is still quite impressive, she said
but how do we find anything there?

Movement 3

finding something in it is not impossible
there are infinitely many numbers and yet
we can study properties of particular ones

but it is better not to walk around there
without a benevolent, illuminated guide
—incidentally you were a terrific guide
in the magic museum this afternoon

i love museums and libraries, she said

the underlying reality contains everything
we can know and every logical possibility

even more interesting than possibilities
are rules or grammars that explain
what is and what is not the case

the underlying reality contains
the set of true arithmetic and
the fact that no function exists
in first order logic to indicate it

... i am not sure i follow, she said

we can think of each field of mathematics
as a platonic object in underlying reality
and each of them is defined by its axioms

mathematics has different buildings but
they all should be connected in some way
some can be transformed into each other
others are the same building, smaller ones
could be contained within larger ones

at the top of the hierarchy there is one
mathematics that encompasses all

this ultimate mathematics is then
the entire content of underlying reality

it is the divine thought
the truth that is in the mind of God

this is beautiful!

platonism is seen as commitment
to just one mathematics

they were silent for some time
listening to the sounds around them
people spoke with subdued voices

a mathematician conjectures a sentence
then asks if the sentence is grammatical
a proof of a sentence is its derivation
from the axioms

the answer to the question
if the sentence is grammatical or not
is a consequence of the properties
of the platonic object being studied

why do we call it underlying reality?
it is underlying of what? she asked

underlying of the material world

there is a material world which
we explore with our senses
we can touch it and see it
and our bodies are part of it

the material word is changing over time
our universe was born, is growing up
its childhood has passed, it is aging
all stars will eventually disappear
even black holes will evaporate

all that is composed will come to an end
the essence of matter is temporality

in addition to the material temporal realm
there is the immaterial atemporal realm
which is the underlying reality

it is more real because it is unchanging

Movement 3

suddenly they perceived piano music
as if coming from another world

they stopped their conversation to listen
they looked around to locate its source
she pointed to an open window
and said, Schubert f-minor sonata

do you play the piano? he asked

i don't know, she replied

you don't know? he asked surprised

i'm confused about musical instruments
these days, she admitted

the music flowed into the night

is there nothing immaterial and temporal?
she wondered

time acts on matter, time acts on energy
but the laws of physics are time invariant
time does not act on the laws of mathematics
the platonic solids do not change over time

what is science? she said

scientists study properties of this universe
they build theories and perform experiments
ultimately the aim of science is to discover
the laws of nature, the mathematical principles
which govern the material world timelessly

the scientists ask questions according to
their premises and nature gives answers
the answers are interpreted in the light
of hypotheses which change over time
but the endeavor can only succeed if
the search space of grammars is limited
—as we have noted before

...of grammars? she wondered

the scientist is a child aiming to learn
the grammar of the temporal material
the mathematician is a child aiming to learn
the grammar of the atemporal immaterial

Einstein said he made progress because
he never stopped asking those questions
which only a child would ask

scientists move from data to theory
mathematical theory tells them what
to measure and how to interpret it

the learning process is inductive inference
humanity grows science in a similar way
as a child grows a language organ
combined humanity has a science organ

science is not a purely objective
description of the material world
because the search process is
guided by the constraints and
subjectivity of the human brain

the same is true of mathematics
she thought

humans produce human science
constrained by that which could be
called universal scientific grammar
as instantiated by the human brain

no learning process that infers rules
from data can succeed without priors
the search space must be constrained

crede ut intelligas, she remarked
believe that you may understand
we are Augustinians of the night!

Movement 3

what if the material world is eternal?
what if the big bang was caused
by an eternal material field which
generates universes in perpetuity?
is this field material and atemporal?
it could be material and everlasting
but if it generates universes at a rate
then it would not be atemporal

one day we may admit all four combinations
immaterial/atemporal — material/atemporal
immaterial/temporal — material/temporal
but for now let us stay with two of them

one by one the people drifted away
and the place became silent

4

let me summarize, she said
it may have been hard to follow

we experience certain dualities
temporal versus atemporal
material versus immaterial

to those we can add:
the instantiated and the divine
the created and the uncreated
the contingent and the necessary

the divine is existence itself
all else receives existence from the divine
all existence is traced back to the divine

the divine is innermost existence
in everything that exists

the uncreated gives rise to the created
the necessary causes the contingent

do you follow me? she asked

i do

the divine action causes existence
another word for action is thought
the divine thought causes existence

Aristotle used *nous* for divine thought
nous can also mean thought or God

the divine thought is good
good is the same as beautiful
true goodness is true beauty
undistracted, unconfused, unveiled
the divine thought is beautiful

the converse is true as well
goodness itself is divine thought
beauty itself is divine thought

are you following me?

i am, he said but he was sleepy

the divine thought is
the most ordered thought

what is the tool that gives us
the most ordered thought?
that allows us to partake
in the most ordered thinking?

it is mathematics, he answered

it is mathematics, she affirmed

the association between beauty
and mathematics becomes clear

the divine thought being the most
ordered is also the most mathematical

since the divine thought wills
into existence all that is instantiated
temporal or atemporal
material or immaterial
mathematics is permeating all
mathematics is everywhere

furthermore the divine thought
wills into existence the human mind,
the human thought, and its faculties
thus we have the ability to understand
mathematics that permeates the world

the divine thought which is in us
and around us is mathematical

it all comes together
the mathematical conundrum is resolved
the ubiquity of mathematics becomes clear
its inexplicable efficiency is explained

do you agree? she asked

i do, he said

she paused

she observed him drifting
between attention and sleep
he needed to sleep so badly

she smiled

then very quietly she asked
do you love me?

he was wide awake

i do, he said, i most certainly do
with every fiber of my existence
i really do! why do you ask?

tend my sheep, she thought

listen to my words, she said
just for a few more minutes

the divine thought is unlimited
the human thought is limited

the limitation of the human thought
is willed by the divine thought

the God-given limitation of human thought
is an appropriate tool for studying the world
the human limitation does not fool us
the human weakness brings us to God
the purpose of our life is the love
expressed within the human limitation

the love which emanates from a fragile
temporal confused...very tired...being
that love is different than the love of God

we need to distinguish between
divine love and human love

the love of the creator is the act of creation
the love of the creation is desire for the creator
love is the desire for the good for the beautiful
love is for the divine

the fulfillment of love is unification
the fulfillment of love is to be one
with the beautiful, with the good

the fulfillment of love is unification
between the creator and the created

love makes provisional dualities vanish
then all becomes one again—the One

do you see this?

absolute monism! the One that is unchanging
the One that does not have existence but is existence
the One whose essence is existence

the incarnation and the logos reveal
the longing of the divine for the instantiated
the love of the creator for the creation

do you get it?

there was no reply

the incarnation and the logos
are expressions of the divine love

it is all so easy, she said

he was fast asleep

God wants to be found by love
the way to God is love

scientific measurement
mathematical proofs
logical arguments
lead to the vicinity of God
but only love provides
the experience of God

only the lover sees truth
undimmed truth which is
beyond logical comprehension

not logic leads to truth but love

she smiled, they say love makes blind
but i say those who do not love are blind

love makes you see the very essence
which is beautiful beyond comprehension
love leads you beyond... nothing else does!

not sacrifice, not duty, not hard work
only love leads you beyond—it is very easy

imagine you love a person
you love her very much

she paused

you love me very much

he was asleep now

hypothetically speaking, she inserted
for the sake of a theoretical exposition

the more you love me
the greater i become in your world
the more you love me
the more encompassing
i become of everything
that is true and beautiful

the more you love me
the less and less
you comprehend me
the less you grasp me
with finite logic
with scientific rigor
with true arithmetic

there is no function that indicates me
no finite system that defines me

you will hear me in music
you will see me in paintings
i will surface in geometry
sculptures will embody me and no other

all activities, all composition
all poetry, all derivation
all joys in life lead to me
and yet... i am beyond them

i am beyond, i am Beyond

you attribute properties to me
which no mortal can have
you see me ruling the world
on behalf of the Divine
aligning it with His goodness
setting it on an unwavering path
that leads to Him forever

you make me First after God

the more i grow in your love
the more unrealistic your esteem of me
in the eyes of the world which is confused
but the more realistic in the eyes of those
who understand, who see beyond
who see the essence of reality

i grow in your love
toward a platonic form
toward the platonic form
which constitutes the Beloved

i become most real
i become immortal
i become atemporal

do you follow me, my friend?

the platonic form is more real
than anything in the material world
which imitates the form

yet the platonic form
is beyond comprehension
you can feel her presence
my presence!

but you cannot hold on to her
you cannot be with her

if there were a mathematical proof
for the existence of the Beloved
that is of God or of me
if there were a scientific measurement
or an inescapable logical argument
revealing my essence—it could not be me

your love would be incomplete

but it is not, i know it is not

she was quiet for some time

now i am telling you everything
that you always wanted to know
and you are asleep, she said

but do not worry
you have not missed it
i will make sure of that

one day you will wake up
and these thoughts will be in you
you may have read them in the library
which we traversed together long ago

and then followed a mere whisper

know this: i am the truth, i am the logos

5

he had noticed two men arriving
he had seen her being called
from the garden in the morning

the conversation had lasted hours
it was dark when the visitors left
he did not know them but assumed
they were high government officials

what had happened?
was her identity revealed?
was she a candidate?
was she the candidate
as he had suspected years ago?
if so what was her response?

these questions were in his mind
when he saw her crossing the yard
and slowly walking toward his house
she seemed lost in thoughts

he heard her knocking at the door
which was always unlocked

he hurried to open for her

he perceived at once
that she was unchanged
that her serene nature
was unperturbed by any news
she might have received

he was relieved and happy
had he ever doubted her?

my good teacher, she said
with warmhearted kindness
would you like to take a few steps
with me on this beautiful evening?

i have some questions...

they walked out of the village
they gained the hill she loved
there was an infinitude of stars
above them and around them

on the top of the hill she sat down
and he followed her lead

then she laid down in the grass
and looked up at the stars
there was no light pollution
the moon had not yet risen
some nebulae were visible

good teacher, have you ever seen
the birth of a star? she asked

this is a rare event, he replied

or the death of a star?

they are almost immortal

once i read a poem about a star
who was in love with a princess
he asked God to make him mortal
he called God "the giver of death"

do you know that poem? she asked
i do not, he answered
a poem you do not know? she teased
could it be in the future?

have you held a star in your fingertips?
she tried out a few...

then she turned to him
her face was suddenly without a smile

have you ever been asked to rule a world?

he did not answer

Movement 3

it seems you have thoroughly
studied my homework

i admit i have, he answered
with your consent i wish to add
you also granted me permission
to read your early written work
from the time before i came here

not to worry, good teacher
i know that all you do is
for the benefit of the world
in you i trust completely
... and i always will

did you really find similarities
between the scribblings of a child
and the work of the first poet
at the dawn of human civilization?

i only made humble guesses
my observations were investigated
by the greatest scholars of the order

also with my consent? she asked

this time he was silent

o my good teacher, do you realize
there would have been another solution
had you done your work less diligently
i could have remained a servant

i could have continued my efforts
in this village as i had planned
our solemn tranquility here
would never have been upset

but instead you uncovered me
as your sense of duty commanded
you turned me into the limelight
you exposed my humble disguise

you removed the cover
that was unknown even to me
you lifted the veil of ignorance
between me and the world

he looked at her in surprise
did she really think there could
have been another choice?

the uniqueness and transparency
of the trajectory was evident to him
hence it must be clear to her too

never mind, she said, the course
of history has to be followed
the world demands heroines
and goddesses but not maids

you traced my footsteps
over the map of time and
you knew me, good teacher
before i knew myself

i am of no significance
o light of my life, he replied
a mere pebble on the shore
you are the ocean of truth

my infinite blessing was to cross your path
whoever is near you if only for a moment
if only in a single life is forever enriched
is eternally uplifted among those stars

an old saying is: whoever listens
to the conversation of the gods
receives the gift of immortality

where are the gods? she said

they were quiet for some time
looking up at the innumerable stars
sensing light particles that came
from a profusion of distant pasts

she looked at the constellation
canes venatici whose name she knew
was a mistranslation in the chain that
led from greek to arabic to latin

she found its brightest star and curiously
recalled its chinese label: *chang chen yi*
first of the imperial guards

there are no gods, she said
there is only God

beyond the village and the forest
the ocean was a hovering infinity
in which the moon would rise soon

my soul too is parsing information
that arises from different times
from different lives, she thought

what is to come now? she asked

memories are born in the past
but the future is unknown to us
this is the essence of temporality
he answered

have you accepted?

i have not, i wanted to talk to you first
what is your advice, good teacher?

o light of the world, it is your decision
no one may dare to influence you

but what is your analysis? she insisted

no person who has ever asked
you for help was rejected by you
now a world is applying

previously you helped a few
now you can infuse yourself
into an entire realm

it is a call for a noble and
selfless action beyond doubt

good teacher, you are right
i reject no one who applies
to me in earnest but still
the vocation ahead is unclear
the men talked about serving
but they really meant ruling
yet the good can never rule
what is good can only serve

the good is measured like this:
a good act in the smallest manner
is of the same value as the good
affecting the whole world

the lowest maid can do the same
amount of good in one moment
as a selfless ruler in her entire life

he looked at her in astonishment
while thinking about this revelation

she continued

you told me that long ago the world
became transparent in a process
which enabled light to travel freely

did he?

the world is transparent for those
looking beyond the veil of confusion
confusion is caused by selfishness
blindness is generated by greed

but remember that only God is good
all people stand directly before God
God is the only source of goodness
the only measure, the only judge

after some time he said

it is the wisdom of this world
to understand at least in part
the principles you are advancing

the office that is being proposed
is regarded the highest in service
the holder is the servant of all

the holder is ready to give herself
for all people, for all creatures
to empty herself for the world

but the holder is also a beacon
for the people to find their way
an oracle of truth providing the
guidance that is urgently needed

a priestess inhaling the vapors
that are emerging from the deep
a seer immersed in the radiance
of the light descending from high
a queen revealing the natural
ever-abiding, all-pardoning law

at that moment they saw a glimpse
of the moon rising out of the ocean
it was the full moon of midsummer
they stopped their conversation

they observed as the moon
ascended in absolute silence
the ocean waves were rolling
in the path of the moonlight

after some time he said
this world is your world
undimmed you shine like the full moon

Fujiwara Michinaga, she thought
here is a poem he does know

she migrated to the tales
and the shores of the lake
was this long ago or only
yesteryear? who knows?

they will remove me from here
yet this simple place is my home
which i love and will always love

yes they will move you away
but this is no concern to you
because the foxes have holes
and the birds have nests
but you are free as the wind

they will put me in a golden cage

your mind cannot be contained

heed not the splendor
that will surround you
it is a sign for the people
a tower for the beacon

you will not regard it your own
you will live there in humbleness
glamor cannot corrupt you
glory has no hold on you

they will adorn you with flawless diamonds
but none of them can be as pure as you

good teacher you speak
as if you know that i will accept

have you made up your mind?

she got up and made a few paces
she looked toward the horizon

there are never choices in life
all apparent choices are provisional
they are part of the confusion

in darkness you do not know the way
in light there is only one path
it is the journey toward God

she followed the moonlight trail
on the surface of the still ocean

then she turned to him
you will come with me
my proven friend of long!

o light everlasting the order of the world
would not admit it: a teacher has influence

it was my fortune to be the teacher of the maid
but the queen of this world i will not see with my eyes

i can ask for you

the order will hasten to send me elsewhere
extinguishing any trace that could be recovered

the order would be deeply embarrassed
in not knowing how to honor your request
you may as well ask for a pebble on the shore

then i will command the order to find you

you could certainly do this but your wisdom
tomorrow if not already today will make you
realize that i cannot be with you

you are in a state of transition
looking forward and backward
in such moments we want to hold on
but afterwards we know the necessity of letting go

an oracle can have no teacher
a beacon shines without obstruction
it is only illuminated from within

you can no longer have any close
attachment to anyone in particular
all creatures are your children now
all people are equally dear to you

to be sure you will be surrounded
by people who sincerely love you
who love you deeply and honestly
who adore you beyond any measure

but you will not have someone
who is on your very own level
your companion, your friend
all the answers must be yours

in this sense you are alone under the stars
but remember God is always by your side
spend much time in prayer and meditation
do not submit to any confusion

in splendor and honor there is always
less than what meets the eye
all material glamor is only superficial
it has no enduring consequence

then after some time he added
in a long series of sacrifices
that will be demanded of you
this is the first: to let go of me

you talk as if i am the only one
who is sacrificing here, she replied

i have long expected this moment
i have lived toward it fully knowing

your light will always shine for me
any word you have ever said to me
i will hold in my memory forever

you were the teacher not i
but this world is your world
this world is waiting for you

after some silence she said
what will you do without me?

the order will send me places
i have been an agent of the search
but now the search is over
they will find other tasks for me
they will send me to remote locations
where no chance encounter occurs

i am infinitely grateful for the journey
which we have made together

it has changed me forever
you have transported me
from this world to another

i will treasure those years
and moments in my heart
my life is devoted to God

she looked at him
there were tears in her eyes

he realized he needed courage for
the next few words he had to say

this is a good place to part
this place has always been magic for us
it is better here than elsewhere
it is better now than tomorrow

brief is the farewell for a long friendship

it was more than a friendship, she thought

she looked at him in silence
as the moon gained height

his eyes were lowered

she considered hugging him
she realized they never had

but instead she said
i hold you in highest possible esteem
i do not admire any man more

6

imagine the appearance of the world
if you have learned to see beyond

if you remove the veil of confusion
you can behold infinite beauty
then for the first time you can see
the true self that resides in all people

walking through a city you marvel
at the unveiled beauty of passersby

you no longer judge them
by superficial appearance
you see the depths within

imagine the sense of wonder
that you now behold in every
pair of eyes looking at you
you see God in all of them

imagine a world that is unconfused
a world transported beyond greed
a world directed by what is good
if you love God you see beautiful
mystery at every street corner

realizing how the world truly is
everything becomes meaningful
that is infinitely meaningful
because God gives meaning

the purpose of life is
to fall in love with God

falling in love with God
implies falling in love with His creation
with the instantiated world
with the underlying reality
with the logos, with truth
with the laws of nature
with mathematics, with people

falling in love with God
means participating in His creation

miracles are not traced by science
they elude traps of measurement
since every moment is a miracle
it is a miracle when people meet
when their worlds touch

some meetings are brief others enduring
but all have significance

every encounter is a miracle
every friendship is a miracle
every word of love is a miracle

the wonder of trajectories
intertwining and embracing never ends

the visible universe is the sphere
from which love reaches us

there is also the sphere
into the smallest scales
the cells of our bodies
the molecules of those cells
the atoms of the molecules
the elementary particles
the force fields, their flavors
their parities, their symmetries
the Planck length

we are suspended between
the exceedingly large and
the unfathomably small
we are in the middle

science makes the world mysterious
philosophy makes it rational
theology makes it shine

in addition to those spheres
those lenses into the largest
and the smallest of scales
there is an unbounded world
within each one of us

use your one pointed mind
to illuminate that world
explore it and be surprised
you find underlying reality
you gain meaning within you

as you mover deeper inside
as you come closer to your
own center...you find God

God who is innermost
existence in each of us
who lifts each one of us
from nothingness to being

the wonder that extends
from you to the outside
must also reach within

know yourself and you find God

the world within freed from worries
becomes a universe of infinite beauty

selfishness causes opaqueness
which prevents light from traveling
once selfishness has dispersed
the mind becomes transparent
then thoughts can travel freely

those thoughts are no longer particular
no longer idiosyncratic, no longer yours
they are everyone's, they are God's

become a traveler toward the center
toward God

once selfishness has gone
all worries disappear
and what is left is God

this is nirvana

this is what makes this life your last

7

you are in my eyes
you are in my thoughts
you are in my mind

then where am i not?

in my fate

the perfect love
is what you wish for
but in this world
you strive for the form
without ever reaching it

this world is about
longing not achieving

they reached a street corner
where they needed to part
it was almost dawn

here? he asked

over there, she said, pointing
to a place under a tree
whose flowers filled the air
with a fragrance of hope

she turned to him and said
thank you for this moment

for this moment?

for the moment we had together
for meeting me walking with me
your words have transported me
from this world into another

your ideas, your insights, your love
have illuminated dimensions for me
have brought glimpses of truth
and recalled everlasting memories

he was moved from one dream
to another—one he liked less

this is no surprise, she continued
it was clear from the beginning

what i am cannot be with only
one person but has to be with
all people, belongs to the world

do you agree?

he looked at her

your confusion is almost gone
she continued, there are only
a few clouds left which will
disperse after a summer rain

i am confident that you have
the ability to see beyond this
one last remaining distraction

... one day, she thought

if not today then tomorrow
if not tomorrow then soon

sometimes i think i can see beyond
then again i am without hope, he said

this struggle is what life is about
she replied her eyes full of compassion

life is a journey, a progress toward
a state where opaqueness dissolves
where you see the absolute as it is

without hope people are blind
it is hope that makes you see
you are almost there, she said
this was my gift to you
over those past few months
do you realize this?

your gift was invaluable to me
but i do not know where i am

she smiled with great kindness
what was once read to us?

you mean what was read
to us in that small church?

yes do you remember?

"do not worry"

do not worry, she repeated

he was silent

silence drifted by

he fought to control emotions

then he asked
is this audience really finished?

am i a queen who gives audiences?

i do not know, he answered
you are a sovereign of the heart
not only of mine of course

suddenly she hugged him
holding him she whispered
if you ask me to be yours
i will not reject you

but i will not be the same
i will be a different person
i will be someone else
do you understand this?

he did not reply

do you want to be with me
or with someone else?

Movement 3

i want to be with you!

then you have to let go
do you realize this?

maybe i do, but i wish i did not

the choice is yours, she said

what will it be?

he was silent

daybreak was close by now
then suddenly the vocalization
of a single bird hung in the morning air
others joined one after the other

the choice is yours, she repeated
in this midsummer night's dream
whose candles have burnt out

what will it be?

he was silent

she heard his heart beating
her compassion tore her apart

the night turned into a pale morning
which was still void of any color

color would come for some today
he thought, but not for me

she repeated her question
do you want me to be who i am
or do you want me to be another?

who you are, he answered

who i am, she said

exactly who you are, he said

exactly who i am, she repeated

very slowly she let go of the embrace

is this how love ends? he asked

love never ends
love has a beginning
but it has no end

the love that illuminates the first moment
is the same love that shines in all eternity

if you look deep into your heart
you see this choice is yours not mine
because this world is your world

my world?

you cannot keep me for yourself
you must share me with all

i know

it is more blessed to give than to receive
your offer here is given and received

after a long silence he asked
by which name may i remember you?

what is the significance of a name?
she smiled, the true self that resides
in every creature is nameless

again she looked at him
with great love and compassion

she made a few steps away from him
but then stopped and came back

she whispered, i want you to know this
as for being in love i am, i truly am

and was gone

8

next morning she rose early
she wanted to wash the floors
in that little shelter once more
as she had done often before
her resolve was to do them
when no one would see her

she did it on her knees
but she was disturbed
by the pending farewell

she implored God to protect
the people in this village

then she went to morning prayer
where she was cold as usual
yet her burning heart was on fire
her outpouring love was unquenchable

in thee abide fixed forever
the first causes of all things unabiding...

afterwards she wanted to finish
the work in her garden of Eden

she drank water at the fountain
how old was this well?
who gave it to the people?

... will you give me a drink?

how can you ask me for a drink?

if you knew who i am
you would ask me for water

you have nothing to draw with
and this well is deep

*if you drink the water of this well
you will be thirsty again
if you drink the water that i offer
you will never be thirsty again*

give me that water . . .

while working she noticed
the birds sitting in the trees
and on the rooftops catching
the rays of the morning sun
they were of different species
but they knew each other
as friends and companions

when the sun rose
the morning gained color

her work was a prayer
of gratitude and admiration
every moment was a wonder
of infinite expanse

after a few hours her work
in the garden was finished

one of the milkmaids came
she was the one who had
loved the garden the most
she was willing to take it over

where are you going?
the milkmaid asked

i do not know

but you are leaving?

i am

she gave her a few explanations
for the garden but the tasks were
so simple that none were needed

Movement 3

the conversation lasted a few minutes
then the garden had a new steward

in the end they hugged
hiding their emotions

she looked at the sky
and realized it might rain
she longed to feel that rain

where would they take her?
to another garden, another world?
would it rain there too?

was there a coming back?
would she visit the village?
as a spirit? a time traveler?

again she yearned to stay
she wished not to abandon
those who were entrusted to her

why always moving?
why always letting go?
why the endless journey?

she looked at the houses
the people at work
the children at school

then she noticed the men had returned
they were expecting her in the same room

she went there and knocked
two had left but three had come

their faces revealed suspense
they bowed deeply to greet her
she was surprised no longer

we wish you a glorious morning

may God bless you, noble lords

is this the day of decision?

you will receive my answer

did you have enough time
to consider the application?

there are many moments in an hour
and many hours in a night of prayer

do you have any further questions?

my deliberations are finished

there was a pause after this answer
which had not been expected

most respectfully, madam
may i ascertain that you appreciate
the magnitude of the decision

i do

do you understand that a world
is appealing to you?

i do

and the answer you are about
to give comes from your heart
is based on your love for God
and for the entire world
while no one is exerting
undue influence over you?

the decision is my own
after careful evaluation

and you have no attachment
to anyone in this or any realm?

she was silent for some time

i am attached to all people

that is, madam, i presume
equally attached to all people
but not specifically attached
to any one person in particular?

Movement 3

she thought of her teacher
then of Lina, then of God
who is the same God in all

she answered, my love is for God

after more silence and realizing
that they had wished her response
to be more precise she added

i have no specific attachment
to any one person in particular

her voice was at the verge of breaking

madam, neither here nor in any realm?

what does he mean?

after some time she replied
not here, not anywhere

then may we renew our appeal?

please do

it is our sacred duty to convey
to you the following question:
in the name of the committee
in the name of the government
in the name of the people you love
do you accept to serve and
to extend the unbroken line?

she looked at all three men
from one to the other
then toward the window

she noticed that the morning sun
was about to illuminate the room

was she still free as the wind?
free as the birds in the trees?

her first thoughts reappeared
they were of God, of prayer
of love for people around her

the door that was opened
the food, the warm bed

the first days at school
appeared in somber twilight
imposing tall demands
that were hard to meet

then Lina and Lina
from the playground
from the trees
from the village
torn away
the first soul
the greatest soul
the pain that never ended

nights in prayer, the first meditation
coming of age, emptying out

the ever-growing light within
from whence did it shine?
were there holes in the canopy of the world?
what was her calling under the stars?

the arrival of the teacher
how he cared for her!
how he stilled her questions
and led her to new ones

the books she read at night
the awakening of memories
which were unrecognizable
as the living water within

the thoughts everlasting
going earlier and earlier
further and further
beyond the veil of ignorance
beyond confusion
beyond any limit

her burning heart was on fire
she was a child no more

the meditations deepened
the prayers became more fervent
letting go became feasible

her love, her life was service
she asked for nothing in return
her internal world expanded
her inner horizons overtook
any observable universe

she discovered time within

she was far now
far from the scene
far from the moment

yet deep in the moment
immersed in eternity

she was the moment
she was the eternity

her thoughts returned to
the world that was waiting
that wished to be loved

she noticed that the three men
were still expecting an answer
for a while she thought
she had already given it

the answer was so obvious
what were they waiting for?

clearly she was the servant of God
the servant of the people

she collected herself and said

i accept

there was another tremble
in the fabric of space time
in the program that hovered
over the limitless tape

the machine that could call
upon an oracle had its answer

the oracle had spoken
the word was accepted
it belonged

her mind slipped again into
the vast expanse of emptiness
she looked far into the future
she surmised events to come
both known and unknown

she looked beyond the three men
who were now kneeling before her

the sun fell into the room
marking the light of a new era
the furniture was simple
in the style of the last but one queen
in the line that was never to break

her outfit was poor

the scene became the inspiration
of innumerable representations
of art throughout the centuries
many painters focused on the light
of the new epoch but none were able
to capture the disarming simplicity
of her modest appearance

after a long silence
the third man who had
not spoken so far asked

which name do you choose?

MOVEMENT 4

1

from a distance
a young guard
was looking on
over the palace
over the gardens
with magnificent trees
pavilions, ponds, bridges of jade
terraces facing a southern ocean

suddenly he saw
the appearance
translucent in outlines
suffused by the light
of the silvery moon

her movements
her reflective steps
her halcyon solitude
her gaze toward horizons
beyond the ocean of truth
beyond the stars where time was born
beyond any confines of temporality

made him surmise
that it was the woman herself
who had come out to ponder
her fate under the heavens

she was engaged in thoughts
wondering what it was that
moved her along the steps
of the trajectory of existence

where did words come from
that structured her thinking?
that quivered her vocal cords?
how did knowledge arise?

every moment was a miracle
was she real or imaginary?
a reverie in someone's mind?
or an idea in that of God?

who made her thoughts?
why did they obey her?

Descartes was sure of two things
that he existed, that God existed

where does reality begin?
where does dream end?
was she a platonic form
transported into this world?

in that case was she more
real than anything material?
or less so? why less so?
are there degrees of reality?

could empiricists derive her
from physical appearance?

do realists know her without seeing her?
or do they see her without knowing her?

was she herself a realist or an empiricist?
was this even a pointed dichotomy?

Movement 4

she now walked through the garden
as a morning breeze came from the sea

a hidden staircase led down
the cliffs to the waters below
she had descended it
with her consorts to swim
in the morning dawn or evening sun
and even at night when only starlight
bounced off the waves

now a tune was in her mind
singing of distant memories
when flowers were in bloom
and when love was innocent

she saw a tame swan whose
plumage matched her garment
she looked for the sumptuous
peacock who was partial to her

she observed a female rabbit
watching over her young ones
she noticed golden and blue birds
building nests in the budding trees

those were the legendary trees
both of life and of knowledge
they knew her thoughts and
held on to her spoken words

were memories real or imaginary?

imaginary numbers were first seen
by mathematicians of the renaissance
their presence in the world was felt
before their understanding crystallized

she thought of Sandro Botticelli
of Primavera, of the golden sandals
she wore on the soft forest floor
and of reaching the shore in spring

how hard he had labored
on these accents of light
in the grass, in the trees
on the wings of the winds

how unnatural her body had seemed to her
when it was all done but she loved her eyes

there was a sadness in those eyes...
...of letting go...of always letting go
of never belonging...of never holding

the one fundamental experience
of her life is that of letting go

then she thought of Ovid
who had loved her dearly
and...whatever he wrote for her
however hard he kept trying for prose
everything became a verse...

ver erat aeternum
it was eternal spring

in school she was asked
to translate his verses which
—unknown to her and others at the time—
had been composed for her

she looked over the waves of the ocean
in their great timeless continuity

eternity was not a sequence of moments
the present moment and eternity were one

sublime happiness overcame her
she looked at the immoveable spot
under the beloved ancient bodhi tree

tonight she will spend in meditation!

the gardens had grown over centuries
and yet they seemed created for her

Movement 4

what is time passing in this palace?
what in the library? in the museum?

what time is needed for an origin of life?
for the inflation of a universe?
for the evaporation of a black hole?

unseen buddhist monks raked the gardens
and kept them in immaculate condition
other people were invisible to them

she wondered if they heard her words

the trees made the winds
the winds made the words
the ocean revealed the truth
unlimited and unsurpassed

her desire was to serve
her love was offered to all
her aim was to lead people
beyond the veil of confusion

renouncing selfishness would make
them ultimately free and unconfused

in some distance she now saw
one of her consorts looking
toward her respectfully
as if posing a question
was any service required?

she encouraged her to approach

the consorts seemed in possession
of miraculous otherworldly powers
they were aware of her intentions
they were in place when needed

they were aligned with her
they organized everything
she was supposed to do
they helped with every task
she was never without them

they were matched in appearance
wearing the same outfits as she did

any moment they could make
her vanish amongst them
utilizing the intended similarity

it was a defense procedure
from old unenlightened days
it was no longer needed now
when it represented a tradition

their number she did not know
some she recognized by now
each one was oriented toward
her with love and devotion

it was her aim to get to know
all of them and be their friend

she now recognized Ariane
whom she had seen more than others

Ariane came close and fell on her knees
a custom she had wanted to stop at once
when she first saw it but then she realized
it was for their benefit and not for hers

it was a part of their nature
it was what they longed for
what aligned them with her
it created the inner harmony

she raised her and hugged her
they were of the same height
they looked very much alike
she held her in close embrace

Ariane started to sob quietly
she thought she understood
and gently caressed her hair

be calm, all is good, she said

Movement 4

she moved out of the embrace
glanced at her and whispered
Ariane, look into my eyes!

Ariane tried for a moment
but did not succeed
her eyes were wet

Ariane tried again and gave up

then very gently she kissed
Ariane on her mouth

immediately Ariane sank down
wept uncontrollably
prostrated herself on the stone floor
which was warm in the morning sun
and pressed the face
against the hem of her gown

3

the goddess had revealed herself in the vedas
which have neither beginning nor end

the goddess had explained she was the form
that existed before the creation of the universe
and that will still exist after its destruction
the form which brings forth life and evolution

the goddess had decreed as follows

Brahma, you are the generator of the universe
i will be your consort—as goddess of wisdom
and of science i embody cosmic consciousness

Vishnu, you are the preserver of the universe
if there is life you take different incarnations
from your mystic sleep i become the goddess
of joy and exaltation—your faithful consort

Shiva, you are the personification of time
you destroy and regenerate all compounds
when you are formless time stands still

you have been meditating on me eternally
as your consort i surpass my other forms
i exclude evil, uphold love, truth, beauty,
and the unity of all gods to be one God

thus the goddess had spoken in the vedas
which have neither beginning nor end

4

tomorrow is your instantiation
and this is a special night
this is the last night before
you enter a new circle of light

according to custom of old
i am coming to you now
to offer my support and
to pray with you in this hour

he paused

if a regret is in your heart
or any bitterness regarding
someone who has hurt you
inadvertently or deliberately
you are invited to let go of it

tomorrow you are the servant of all
the arbitrator of the world—then you
cannot hold misgivings toward anyone
you cannot be biased against a soul

my good father, you and your brethren
have expressed great kindness to me
over these past weeks and months

you have diligently prepared me
for this moment and i am enlightened
by your company, piety, and wisdom

once again i say unto you:
if anyone has wronged me
in this realm or in others
i hold nothing against them
i forgive them before God

i release them from any debt
they may have accumulated
all failure is only ignorance
i embrace anyone who may
have trespassed against me
knowingly or unknowingly
i embrace them with the love
which it is my desire to uphold

likewise if i have hurt someone
if i was blind to their concerns
or did not sufficiently participate
in their hardships or joys i beg
them to forgive me before God

after some silence he said

and most humbly, madam
since i have the permission
to speak in your presence
i kindly ask you to consider
if there are any actions of yours
any thoughts past or present
which cause you concern

she reflected then she said
meet me in the chapel

he bowed and withdrew

entering the chapel
she saw him kneeling
in front of the altar
she walked toward him
and knelt down by his side

they prayed in silence

then she said quietly
there is a poor heart
which i have incited in love
which i have left behind
in the world from which i was taken

Movement 4

after a moment he answered

i am informed we worked diligently
to remove any painful sentiments
new responsibilities were presented

the human soul sometimes
needs the solitude of winter
in order to delight again
with the flowers of spring

there is no lingering pain
for someone devoted to God

again there was silence

good father, i hear your words
and i follow your perspective
yet i feel there is a loving soul
walking the earth missing me

silence

forgive your humble servant
who ventures to speak to you
as you know the incarnation
of the form is only illuminated
from the light cast within
there cannot be attachment
nor dependency of any kind

i know, there cannot be, she replied

do you feel any such obligation?
has your heart made a commitment?

she considered for some time

i am unable to gain transparency

he was silent

eventually he asked

if there were a conceivable commitment
would you be willing to renounce it?

i would not

he was surprised by her response
but he knew better than asking again

does this constitute an impairment
for my ability to serve? she asked

i do not know since the core of
the program is hard to evaluate
he answered

they were both silent

the room was lit by a single candle
lux aeterna

the flickering light danced on her face
her eyes were closed, her internal image
was of the golden cross in front of them
which too reflected the light of the candle
the eternal sacrifice, the perpetual offering

good father, there is a conundrum
which i am unable to resolve

how could i make a choice
which implies sadness for someone
which causes a soul to feel loss?

if being in my presence is a
blessing and leads to better
understanding of the form
then how can i take a step
which removes someone
from my company or makes
it harder for them to see me?

if here i am asked to be a servant
of all people but there i withdraw
my proximity from a single loving
soul then something is severed
in the edifice of this universe

Movement 4

and perhaps i am not even
talking of a single soul alone
i am concerned for the village
from which i was removed
who knows how many people
are missing me in this place?

i cannot sacrifice the happiness
of another person for the sake
of the whole world—i can only
sacrifice myself—do you agree?

he considered

she was aware of the faintest
sound the candle made while
burning her own body to light

i fully concur, he answered
if you are true to yourself
if you are true to your mission
you cannot cause anyone to suffer
you cannot give up anyone else
for the world, the only oblation
that you can seek is your own

the eternal law in this temporal realm
is that self-sacrifice leads to salvation
this principle ought to guide you

whomever fate has brought
in your path you cannot abandon
you must shine equally for all souls

withdrawing your light from anyone
is a punishment that is not permitted
no punishment is compatible with
the goodness, forgiveness, and love
that comes from God continuously

before every action you can incentivize
people to do what is right but then
if they have failed you can only forgive
and renew your effort to prepare them
for their next step and hope this time
they will choose to do what is good

it could seem the world is asking
much of you to behave in this way
perpetually but it is not because
you claim nothing for yourself

ask for nothing receive everything!
the law reveals how the good acts
in this world: it asks for nothing
and it never abandons anyone

the good illuminates the path
but people take their own steps

moreover know this, he continued
what is good for a single soul
is good for the entire world
instead of conflict i see alignment

in moving the world the principle
you must apply is the following:
patiently show them the light
and they will see eventually
there is only temporary opacity
but in the end everyone will see

a final revelation: when it comes
for you to take decisions, to chose
between two options, remember
these choices are only provisional
they are apparent, they are not real
there is only one single trajectory
that is taken by the everlasting light

light travels all trajectories
but they cancel each other
until a single one remains
which minimizes time, she thought

when all confusions are gone
only a single path remains
which maximizes goodness

please forgive your servant who is
speaking to you thus, he continued
the words i am finding are caused
by the illumination that comes from
being in your presence before God

if there is any truth in what i say
it is not mine but God's, he added

she was astonished by his wisdom
he seemed wise beyond his age
she did not know his name
whether she had seen him before
whether she would see him again

she now considered taking
a brief glance aside at his face
but then deemed it inappropriate
oh those fleeting interactions...

she explored herself if she had
additional concerns or regrets

*bedenke wohl das Herz ist ein Betrüger
aber nichts berückt das Flammenauge
das ins Innere blickt...*[11]

after some time she said
my heart is revealed to you
my confession is ended

let us finish in prayer, good father
then i invite you to take a few steps
with me outside in the garden

after some reflection he prayed

your goodness o Lord shines
forth over the entire creation
you have chosen your servant
to be consecrated tomorrow
to represent to us the lucidity
which only comes from you

your servant knows that no one is
good in comparison to you, o Lord
that no one stands before you
without the need of forgiveness

only you can see her heart
you alone are her judge
strengthen her on the path
which leads to you forever
o wellspring of all love

forgive her three sins

you have chosen your servant
for the most exalted office
no one is her equal on earth
bless her and support her
in this night, tomorrow
and to the end of all time

after he had finished praying
he rose and left the chapel

she remained in prayer for a while
then too got up and walked outside

the evening was calm

she walked to the edge of
the terrace and leaned over
deep below the waves were
thundering against the cliff

Movement 4

the first stars were visible
she noted the *alpha virginis*
which is a blue subgiant
actually a binary system
with the two stars so close
that they orbit in a few days
the system will resolve
in a type-two supernova

she recalled temples built long ago
that were oriented toward that star

she turned and saw the priest
waiting in a deferential distance
she invited him to approach
by bowing to him respectfully

he did and to her astonishment
even he knelt down before her

venerable priest, she said
pointing to the stars behind her
are you kneeling before me
or the diamond of virgo?

do not kneel before me
instead walk by my side
as in the village my teacher
has done on many occasions

madam, it is an honor in this world
that no one can claim anymore

this world does not fail to surprise me
i bestow the honor on you now and
i will grant it to others in due course

she shivered slightly as a cooler
evening air engulfed them

she had not perceived any of
her consorts on the terrace
but she knew they were always
in watchful attendance

now two of them approached
carrying a fine silk cloth
which they offered to her
she accepted it with gratitude
reverently they put it on her
then they bowed and left
their steps were noiseless

my good priest, when i was a child
there was another orphan close to me
we were inseparable and of one soul

then one day she was torn from me
by the fragility of temporal existence
this scar i am carrying on my heart

i imagine her to be with God
and yet i miss her painfully

my good teacher has told me that
the wise do not mourn the dead
but i do—missing out on wisdom

even Jesus wept, he replied

she looked at him

we do not know the role of a soul
in the unfolding of this trajectory
neither do we know the path
that the Lord has intended for us

they walked in silence
while she weighed his remarks
then she continued

after this forming experience
of my childhood the reasoning
was in me that i should not renew
attempts of making close friends

it seemed to me that my entire
trajectory is one of letting go
therefore i thought it might be
better not to entice anyone

Movement 4

when i met him i noticed
his thoughts were beautiful
there was confusion in him
but also unquenchable light

i realized that he knew much
and that he wished to explain
the entire world to me

specifically the world as he saw it
for no one sees the world as it is

his was an idiosyncratic view
colored by a particular perspective
but not unpleasant to me

i was eager to learn
i was pleased to further
my knowledge which is sparse

there is something endearing
in the partial views of the world
which people have presented to me
i see much purpose in them

he was always good to me
often he could not look at me
rarely could he hold my gaze
i thought this made him special
the relation was otherworldly

or should i say our worldly?
she wondered looking at the priest
who walked quietly by her side

slowly he formed an attachment
but i read in him that his love
was true and entirely unconditional
he was grateful for each moment
which we could spend together

he may have seen me as
the moment to which one says
—in all expansion of time—
remain! thou art beautiful

likewise i was grateful for every
moment i could spend with him

the priest did not interrupt her
they had reached a group of trees
with stone benches beneath them

she sat down and invited him
to do as well but he wanted
to remain standing before her

my good priest, please feel free
to sit down on one of the benches
your deference makes me ashamed

he obliged

what then is your opinion?

your heart's judgment cannot be wrong
he experienced the light coming from you
this is the memory which he now holds

this brilliance will remain in him forever
it will lead him to a good and fulfilled life
he may be considered happy in this realm
there is mourning over loss which purifies

the temporal experience which the Lord
has provisioned for us is one of letting go
the fleeting encounters in time seem brief
but they prepare us for the one encounter
which matters and which will never pass

meeting you, loving you has made him ready
to appreciate the love that comes from God
which is available to all souls and which is
entirely transformative in its limitless joy

Movement 4

then he will also realize that any love between
two souls which occurs in this exile is forever
thus he has not lost you and he never will
no love is ever in vain, no love is unfulfilled
all love is forever, is an eternal object, a form

the love between two souls is written
into them and is part of the universe
all love will find its fulfillment in God
there will be an eternal embrace

she evaluated his answer which she
found deep—eventually she remarked

if it is as you say i am comforted for now
but i will consider the matter further

she looked toward the horizon
and noticed another star rising

she had seen it before
surging from other oceans
ascending over other mountains

yet she was ignorant of the
star's name in the present
what are those names?
how short-lived are they!
how impermanent
why do we care for them?

although labeled by other names
it is the same star in different eons
the same book in different realms
the same soul in different worlds

she thought of the priest by her side
why do i long to know his name?
do names give birth to concepts?
do names provide frames for objects
to partake in the temporal trajectory?
was it a coincidence that—with help
from God—Adam named all animals?

she was silent until the unnamed star
had gained some considerable height

and of tomorrow? she asked
what is expected of me then?

he too had followed the rising star
but now that she looked at him
he lowered his eyes again

my consorts and others have
briefed me on the details of
the ceremony but my question
for you is regarding its purpose

what is the meaning of what
ought to happen tomorrow?

even though, he answered
i am but a small cog in a large
organization i am authorized
to speak to you on this topic

yet my information is only partial
it is conceivable that no one has
possession of the complete picture
we are entering unknown domains

tomorrow is a possible alignment
of the eternal and the temporal
a marriage of heaven and earth

tomorrow is an attempt to set
the world on a path of reason
on a trajectory of enlightenment
which leads to the source of all

your first awareness in this realm
was standing in front of a small
door that had no handle outside
that door was opened for you
and you were received into the
village which you transformed

Movement 4

such a door exists to every human soul
and whoever lives inside has to open
the door for you and therefore to God

such a door exists for the collective soul
of the temporal world because the soul
of the individual is the soul of the world

the atman is the brahman, she added

it is as you say

tomorrow the door is open
and you can pass through it
the process of opening the door
began with initiation of the search

for how long has the search
been in place? she asked

the search started centuries ago
when people realized that every
other attempt of societal structure
had failed badly and let them down

all systems fell prey to selfishness
ignorance, greed, and malice
they faltered one after the other

yet they agreed that in everyone is
natural knowledge of the form which
demands unconditional cooperation

they were silent

then he said, love your enemies!

she was startled

an unnamed lover of wisdom proposed
the concept of the search, he continued

the first committee was formed
but in the beginning no one knew
how to implement the basic idea

the order was hesitant to get involved
it had been burnt too often by politics
there were also critics of the process
who held it was a game of glass beads

but others argued that the search
was valuable in itself because
it focused on critical issues

as time passed the rules of the game
the criteria of the search crystallized
but alas no candidate could be found
until very recently—as you know

just a moment please, she said
the phrase was presented to me
of extending the unbroken line
the wording does suggest a long
sequence of previous candidates

madam, pray forgive me, he pleaded
there is an unbroken line of kings
and queens, of emperors, empresses,
priests, bishops, prophets, and sages
and for sure in this realm have been
many spiritual or temporal rulers
who were ardently devoted to God

some are even called "great"
in the considered yet disputed
judgment of discerning history
but those rulers came about
by means of the old system
largely based on competition
while ignoring cooperation

he was silent

she noticed a group of dolphins
which were traversing the waves
sprinkled with reflections of stars

Movement 4

but she was not distracted
she was focused on his narrative
in fact it began to dawn on her
what he would relate next

as for having been identified
as a target of the search
you are the first one now
you are the only one so far
you are preceded by no one

some prophecies argue that in every age
there is only one suitable candidate
one temporal manifestation of the form

in consideration of such opinions
you will not be succeeded by anyone
and all we have is a single attempt

she shuddered

only one attempt for reaching
a new domain of life? she asked

if the servant is unconfused
then everything is possible, he said

and if the servant is confused
who could carry such a burden?

much is given to you, madam
even more will be asked of you

follow me, she heard him say

who are you? she asked suddenly

a priest like many others, he replied

there is another opinion, he continued
what lives in you is present in all people
what is fully awake in you is a sleeping
possibility available to each one of us
the veil of confusion of selfishness is thin
lifting the veil is possible for everyone

then your burden becomes light, he added

then my burden becomes light, she repeated

it is conceivable that there exists another
human soul whose veil has been lifted

she looked at him

i am not talking of myself

one other secret i can reveal to you:
the door to the world soul and the door
to a single human soul is the same door

what do you mean? she said
am i in need of further explanation
to parse this hidden prophecy?

with deep respect, madam, he said
all pieces of the puzzle are before you
the uniqueness of the entire trajectory
is tied to the uniqueness of each soul

who are you? she asked a second time

madam, i am a servant of your servants
moreover one who has spoken too much
i most sincerely beg for your forgiveness

she sighed

she looked out toward the horizon
for a brief moment she had felt not alone
but now she was alone again

der Erde Gott verlerne zu bedürfen[12]

she composed herself

good priest, i thank you for your thoughts
please go now and return to your prayers
in this night which is truly blessed

Movement 4

please pray for the entire world
which ardently longs to be healed
please pray for me that my love
is acceptable to the One who is Love
please pray especially in this night
for all who are alone, who are sick
who are mourning, who are confused

he rose and again he wanted to kneel
before her but her eyes now fixed on his
commanded him to refrain from doing so

and he obeyed

he bowed respectfully and walked away
she watched him receding in the night

i will never see him again, she thought
not in this realm as they will ensure
in their vast immeasurable wisdom
that i am free from any attachment

she glanced over the ocean
which was nearly motionless
an infinite ocean of existence
from which all things originate

he who existed in the form of God
did not consider equality with God
something to be grasped but emptied
himself taking the form of a servant

she remained seated for a while
she felt completely empty now
but she knew what her purpose
and call were under the heavens

she got up and walked toward
the immovable spot under the tree
she adopted the lotus posture

free from attachment…

she closed her eyes
she observed her thoughts
which were arriving from afar
from beyond the horizon
and even from distant stars

then she let go of them

the world within expanded
the infinite sphere inverted
steadily it grew outwards
toward the other sphere
the observable universe
in which center she rested

the light of the rising moon
fell through her closed eyelids
the tree released its flowers
covering the space around her
in spots of white moonlight

any movement of the air ceased
even the great ocean fell silent

she moved deep and deeper
she remained unchallenged
hour after hour of the night

when the sun finally rose
she had shattered the shell
of any remnants of finite self
that might have been in her
she had removed all opaqueness

she awoke a Buddha

had she ever known
any worries
any selfish desires
she no longer did
not now
not on this day
not in this orbit of time

she was ready

5

he visited the places associated
with sublime happiness now lost
he traced the steps of their walks

he found the garden of awakening
he made a habit of going there
every year on Easter sunday
but no one said *noli me tangere*

he looked for her in the city
at the staircase and in hidden yards
sometimes he caught glimpses of her
walking in a street or sitting in a cafe
but in the end it never was her

he floated alone in the ponds
with the willow trees touching
the surface of the water

the trees still made the wind
but she was not in the trees
nor was she in the wind
the rivers did not flower

there was no other origin of life
life had definitely grown up by now
dreams of emergence, of prelife
and of youth had dispersed

he went to the museum
but it displayed only
the standard collection
there was no stone tablets
referring to Enheduanna
but he did ascertain
the identity of this first poet
named in human history

he traveled to Florence
to see the Botticellis
the paintings had all
details he remembered
he read learned essays
of art historians discussing
the identity of the model
but found them inconclusive

once he received in the mail
a copy of *The Tale of Genji*
but it came without a note
he never knew who sent it

as the lonely years passed by
he began to feel like a shadow
people did not notice him
he inhabited another world

he was a time traveler sharing
the same locations as others
but not their times

was he cast out for having come
too close to the sun like Icarus?

he stayed in the guest room
of a medieval college
which was empty because of
the break between terms
also there he was alone
with church bells counting hours

in that town he went to a small store
that sold old prints and engravings
he saw an image of two women
intensely looking at each other
holding on to each other for life
surrounded by statues and columns
in a place that looked like a crypt

Movement 4

the image caused a sensation in him
for reasons that were indiscernible
he had the sudden need to sit down
the shopkeeper guided him to a chair
on which fell a spot of afternoon sun

he returned the next day resolved
to buy the print but it had gone

as he grew old there was still
an unquenchable light in him
but he was no longer sure
if he had ever known her

had he really met her? walked by her side?
had he conversed and laughed with her?

he was undecided if they had met physically
or only mentally and which counted for more
he was sure that hers were distinct attributes
of infinity largely unfathomable to mortals

he was ashamed to think of her as human
but he was afraid of God to call her divine

the contents of their discourse
were in him and they expanded
he saw her now in distant places
infusing universes with her goodness
leading worlds and souls that were
fully enlightened as to fully know her

6

the palace was stirring
the city was awakening
in all parts of the world
people were getting ready
no one wanted to miss
the splendid celebration
the birth of a new star

the saffron-clothed Eos
the golden-haired Apollo
nudged her out of meditation
Zephyr and Aura drifted her ashore

she got up made a few steps
but her legs did not carry her

she fell down

the consorts were at hand
to lead her back to the world
and to her elegant rooms
where breakfast was laid out

she delighted in the delicate vapor
of tea which was of the variety
famed for its notes of pure water
mingled with peaches of heaven

a bath was ready
then she was dressed in the robe
that had been chosen for the occasion

the color of gentle ivory
flowed down in simple lines

the golden sandals were the
same that previous empresses
had worn at their coronations
they were a relic of tradition
inherited over generations

Movement 4

they were higher than
what she would have chosen
but still comfortable
the consorts knelt down
to close the straps

she was informed that
the lord high steward
the lady of the grand seal
and the lords of the orders
were assembled and ready
they would be much obliged
if she were inclined to honor
them with her presence

she walked toward the door
through a number of rooms
to enter a grand one where
the peers were expecting her

my noble ladies
my esteemed lords
here is your servant
the handmaid of the Lord
let's to church

❊ ❊ ❊

the grand door of the cathedral
stood open signifying a transition
from one epoch to another

it was opened on two instances
the coronation of an empress
and the funeral of an empress

she was to pass through the door
alone while inside the people
waited in solemn anticipation

it had taken hours to fill the church
months to plan the event
years to bring it about

now there was silence

she was unattended in the great plaza
before the cathedral

the obelisk witnessed the event
the arches were onlookers

were they made of ancient stone
of stubborn brass or rolled-out silver?
or were they made of books?
or numbers containing every story?

which were more everlasting:
metals, stones, books, numbers?

numbers! she thought

the square was deserted of creatures
there were no people, no animals
no birds in the sky... she was alone!

had the fountain crystallized?
did the flow of time stand still?
was she hovering over centuries?
or over the face of the deep?

she heard her heart beating
via sound waves in her body
time was passing within her

how did she get here?
she remembered standing
in front of a small door
which was firmly closed
now she stood in front of a
large door which was open

what was in between?
the people in the village
the trees in her garden
the hours with her teacher
the books of wisdom

Movement 4

and those other memories
of psalms and poems
of the flute, of lost love
of the shores by the lake
of a burning city...

there were many burning cities
not only that one! though this
was the most lamented of all

how often had she failed to protect
the weak along their path of tears
how often was she moments too late
and then tormented by agony

was her repeated failure woven
into the fabric of the universe?

could this ever change? could there
be a moment of glory? of triumph?

those questions arose in her
but there were no answers
there was only the silence
before the great cathedral

in her persistent memories
she found inspiring artists,
painters, musicians, poets

time had brought her in contact
with the fates of many souls

were those memories part
of an ever-unfolding present?
those souls part of one soul?

living forever in the moment
she was the moment
how many lovers and poets
had implored her to remain

verweile doch! du bist so schön!
es kann die spur von meinen erdentagen
nicht in äonen untergehen...[13]

books within the great library
genomes and machines reside
in spaces of the forever present
and so do the souls of all people
each one of them contains traces
of the inextinguishable absolute

what gyrates in those spaces?
evolution exploring chambers
visitors entering the library
writers instantiating books
composers finding scores
objects of art being uncovered
and brought forward into the light

these voyages induce time
in a provisional reality
but the underlying truth
is eternal and unchanging

what is *is*! what is not can never be!
the first thought is and always is
the divine thought is and always is
the divine light is—what is *is*!

she thought of the material light
which traveled from distant worlds
carried by immaterial waves
which arose in the cores of stars
and took their time to reach the surface

then they traversed for thousands
or for millions of years or more
interstellar intergalactic emptiness
occasionally inflected by gravity
until their journey ended in the eyes
of some animal gazing at the night sky
creating neuronal signals in its brain

but there is another organ enabling us
to see the light that comes from God
which needs no time to reach us
because it is generated from within

if you go beyond the veil of confusion
you become a light unto yourself

she thought of the cells in her body
coalescing back in an unbroken line
to the first one on this planet
carrying within it the primordial ocean

animals moving from sea onto land
the many-branched web of evolution
leading accidentally or deliberately
to the human realm of prayer

she thought of the first humans
roaming the savannas of Africa
leaving their footprints in soil
that would or not petrify in time

she thought of language
that enabled them to build
towers, walls, and libraries
which reached for the heavens,
cities, and hopes that were
established to be destroyed

struggles for cooperation
with defection, selfishness,
punishment, revenge, outrage
always lurking in the dark

which book evoked the image
of people perceiving themselves
as standing on top of tall columns
erected on the fates of all others
who came before them?

they were now on top because
all preceding ones had vanished
while later ones had not arrived

but for her the people of the past
and the future were contemporary
and she was in the midst of them

while randomness was a yardstick
for the scientists floating in time
it was not her first tool of choice
since she knew God did not play dice

empires had come and gone
the powerful harmed the weak
until they themselves corroded
and were hurt in cycles of pain

empires had come and gone
but religion alone endured
the quest was always there
the quest for the one light
for the face of the absolute

it was her quest too
it was the quest of reason
the quest of love and humility
the search for a true humanity
which she found all embracing

it was a clear call for action
she was ready for engagement

bring me my bow of burning gold
bring me my arrows of desire
bring me my spear, o clouds unfold
bring me my chariot of fire

she looked at the open gate
which was in front of her
in order to reach it she only
had to cross the deserted square

the task was easy, very easy
even in those golden sandals
if she could enter that door
everything would fall into place

but if time stood still then
how could it be accomplished?

oh if time would start again!
maybe it was not supposed to be
and therefore Shiva had stalled

perhaps there was a violation
of natural law and the program
the recursive logic of reality had
halted in irresolvable inconsistency

in her garden in the village
had time stopped too?
or were the plants growing?
were the berries ripening?
did the tree of knowledge
still offer its delicious fruit?

if you ate from it you would know
eritis sicut deus scientes bonum et malum[14]

evil is not a substance
knowing the difference
between good and evil
enables you to orient
yourself toward the good
as sunflowers face the sun
following her course

evil is not and can never be

she thought of the library
which contained every book
it would also offer one that
described the present moment

did she hold the book in her hand?
if she turned over the present page
would the future finally arrive?

would the next page bring
about a messianic age?

instinctively she knew to wait
for the signal but if time stood
still how could a signal arrive?

time, move!

then the vision changed
the centuries were flowing
but she was not in them

there was no trace of her
in the unfolding of years
no action devoted to her
no derivation attempted
no hope however vague

the great door fell shut
the entrance was walled up
the church turned to desolation

then it started to burn
the cathedral was on fire
not only wooden frames
but also stones ignited
the spires were roaring

those first sounds were
soon chased by others
by more horrific ones
people were screaming
in agony and in despair

people were transpiring
from the glowing stones
like drops of blood

Movement 4

she wanted to rush forward
to quench the terrible flames
but she was not in the program
that ran over the tape
her oracle was not requested

the cathedral was by now
almost razed to the ground
but the fire did not stop
it began to reach out
to the surrounding structures
to the city and to the world

it was the vision of a world
entirely devoid of her
recombination was undone
light no longer passed freely

the new shadows emerging
from flames adopted shapes
became monsters of the deep

the smoke was encircling her
as creatures were pressing in
against her from all sides
she knew she was their target

their wiry outstretched fingers
like piercing daggers of death
were now reaching for her
attempting to destroy her
to undo her once and for all

but they could not...
they could not reach her!
they could not touch her!
they could not declare her irrational

their manifestation was smoke
was composite illusion
while her form was prime
was forever

not like this! she said
time, not like this!

time, move!
but with me in you
carry me along
move through my body
make it fragile, vulnerable
but take me along

it was all quiet

then a bell struck

did time obey her commands?
did time sway to serve her will?

had a sound arrived?
from the past, from the future,
or from an immaterial present?

the bell had struck a single time

a flock of birds suddenly unfroze
in the square and stirred up

the clockwork of time ran again
was it triggered by a bell strike?
or by a regress of movers going
back to the first who is unmoved?

there can be infinite progress
but not infinite regress

rapidly she advanced toward the door
now she was truly on fire to reach it
not for her sake but for the world's

up the stairs, a few more steps...
then suddenly... out of nowhere
she perceived an unexpected motion
toward her... blocking her path!

Movement 4

someone must have hidden
between columns by the gate
waiting for her in an ambush

waiting for her until she was
alone without any consorts
separated and unprotected
vulnerable in passing time

the figure made swift strides
and reached her in an instant
and still... she was unafraid

nothing can harm the self
she was guardian of her soul

she faced him and thought
strike what is mortal!

he stood still but was shaking

she saw a monk whose shape
was of poverty and of want

was there a trace of madness
in his somber features?

he approached her closely
she inhaled his perspiration

she recalled that in this realm
no one was free to draw near
without her explicit permission

then he spoke in a refined voice
which outdid his appearance

i am here to remind you that you
will pass through this gate twice

a *memento mori*?

good father, i know my mortality
i am the servant of the Lord

i am here to remind you that all
people are equal before God

good father, i embrace my humility
i am the servant of the people

now you are young and beautiful
but age and disease spare no one
splendor passes while monks stay
i am here to remind you that you
are dust and to dust you will return

my love—however fragile—is for God
who is my First and my Last, she said

she wanted to give him something
she remembered the golden crucifix
the consorts had put into her hands
she gave it to him and he accepted it

i kindly ask you and your brethren
to pray for me in perpetuity

he bowed and was gone

awaking as from a vision
she advanced toward the door

as she passed the threshold
the great bell struck a second time

slowly she moved forward
her hands were folded
her eyes were lowered
she was an icon of humility

she had forgotten all ceremony
but she followed it instinctively

on either side of the aisle were
her consorts kneeling in prayer
dressed in white, hair covered
she looked like one of them

Movement 4

she advanced further among
the dignitaries of the state
emissaries of other countries
heads of governments
kings and queens
priests and bishops
representing all dominions

she saw without looking

she recalled her teacher's words
in all the glamor of the world
is less than what meets the eye
the highest value is only within

in front of the great altar
in respectful distance from it
was a small wooden *prie-dieu*
which was intended for her

she knelt down

the bell struck a third time

the choirs and organs arose
magnificent hymns resonated
through the cathedral and the world

then the readings commenced

who hath measured the waters
in the hollow of His hand
meted out the heaven with a span
comprehended the dust
of the earth in a measure
weighed the mountains in scales
and the hills in a balance?

before Him all nations are as nothing

❊ ❊ ❊

for my thoughts are not your thoughts
neither are your ways my ways

for as the heavens are higher than the earth
so are my ways higher than your ways
and my thoughts higher than your thoughts

❋ ❋ ❋

if i speak in the tongues of men
or angels but have not love i am
only a resounding gong

if i have the gift of prophecy
and can fathom all mysteries
and all knowledge and if i have
faith that can move mountains
but have not love i am nothing

love is patient, love is kind
it does not envy, it does not boast
it is not proud, it does not dishonor
it is not self-seeking, it is not easily angered
it keeps no record of wrongs

love does not delight in evil
but rejoices in truth
it always protects, always trusts
always hopes, always perseveres

love never fails

where there are prophecies, they will cease
where there are tongues, they will be stilled
where there is knowledge, it will pass away

for now we see a reflection as in a mirror
but then we shall see face to face

❋ ❋ ❋

behold, i stand at the door and knock
if any man hear my voice and open the door
i will come in to him and sup with him and he with me

❋ ❋ ❋

Movement 4

she knelt all the time
her eyes were closed
she was in deep prayer

then came the gospel reading

Jesus said to her, Mary...

her eyes opened for an instant
then closed again in acceptance

...she turned toward him and cried "Rabboni"
he said, touch me not for I have not ascended
to the Father...

who had selected that reading?
who chooses in this trajectory?

an old priest dressed in white
celebrated the eucharist
he was assisted by bishops
who were his superiors in office
though not in spirit

ecce homo

ecce agnus dei
qui tollis peccata mundi

she looked up for the first time
the cup of my body is empty

they carried a cross to her
with ardent love she kissed
the feet of her God

she remembered the drop of blood
that had fallen from the cross
onto her lips and into her mouth
in the moment of His death

then she received the blood
and the body of Christ
from the priest who presided

several choirs lifted in unison
Mozart's "Ave Verum Corpus"
into the vast dome of infinity

Ave, ave verum corpus
natum de Maria virgine
vere passum immolatum
in cruce pro homine
Cujus latus perforatum
unda fluxit et sanguine
esto nobis praegustatum
in mortis examine
in mortis examine[15]

when the voice of God had
ebbed away it became silent

she knew it was the moment
she knew it was now or never

once again she prayed
Lord, I am not worthy
to be your servant but
your will shall be done

she stood up the first time
since the Mass had started
she saw that the entrance
to the crypt was wide open

she walked to the entrance
passed through the door
and proceeded down the stairs

she noticed the humidity
arising from the catacombs
it was gloomy and dark
her eyes had to adjust

she saw the sarcophagi
of queens and kings
of the unbroken line
of apostles, of popes,
of prophets and saints

Movement 4

she passed the coffins of two empresses
and noticed a small spot between them
this would be entirely sufficient one day
when time had run its course, she thought

she saw a light at the end of the hall
and she knew to advance toward it

there was a narrow door to another room
which was octagonal and in the middle
on a circular table illuminated from above
or from within—was the crown

the crown for the empress
who was to rule the world
who was to set this realm
on a trajectory toward God
which would never falter

she approached it slowly

a few last steps led to the altar
upon which the crown rested

her arms moved forward to reach for it
arms that reached for crowns of kingdoms

then she noticed the thick glass dome
that was impregnably shielding the crown
her fingers touched the smooth surface
while below the crown was unreachable

she was searching for a mechanism
to release the cover but found none
she looked for a clue, for a hint
was there a lever or a contraption?
why had no one told her? she was puzzled

then the meaning dawned on her
she was not the chosen successor!
there must have been a glitch in the
procedure, a mistake in the program

she was not the target of the search
the search must have misconcluded
maybe it was a probabilistic algorithm

she was not the choice of God
she was not disappointed now...
not in the least... had she been
she would have been unworthy

but the great door was open
the trajectory was prepared
there had to be a candidate

she even felt a sense of relief
the sacrifice that she had freely
offered had not been accepted
her life was again hers to live
as she pleased, she was free
as the wind roaming the land

a deep joy suddenly filled her

she could go back to the world
where she had left a heart behind
where her work was unfinished
she could take basic and simple jobs
she could volunteer for the poor
she could lead an unimportant life
and therefore an important one

moreover she would care for him
when he became old and weak
he could die in her arms
engulfed by her love and prayers

she was mortal again
her heart leaped with joy
she might find the way back
she would find him, comfort him
his sadness would end
she could fulfill his longing
she could be flesh and blood to him
not mere spirit

Movement 4

she could laugh with him
walk with him, cry with him

then she felt sad for the people
the world that was waiting above
in the cathedral of the coronation
had she let them down?

was there something wrong
with her vague recollections?
was there something within
her that had deceived all?
was she herself deceived?

the system in the vault cannot err
she was not the legitimate candidate
once the real candidate was found
the joy of the people would be even
more complete than it was now

all those thoughts arose
within her in an instant
and all were subdued
by her state of emptiness
which still predominated
wavering only imperceptibly
like a tall building in the wind

she listened

there was no noise descending from above
in the cathedral all was as quiet as death

...death!

this was a place of death!

why do they keep the crown among the dead?
because the dead longed for it in their lives
fought for it in their vanity and died for it
misled by the empty promise of its glory

she touched the glass dome once more
it was solid, immovable, uncompromising
she turned to go back without the crown

then suddenly she had the sensation
that she was not alone in the room

she turned slowly, looking around
columns of marble, statues of marble
some of them were illuminated
others were impenetrable shadows
with even darker spots in between

the statues of the empresses
and emperors of ancient times
some of them looking fierce
others powerful and determined
but what was the one real power?
what was the force that counted?

then in the shade of a column
she had the vague impression
as if perceiving a black shape
which was not a lifeless statue
... but a hooded person!

staring intensely at the shadow
of shadows she forgot to breathe

then the figure moved slightly
and subtle light fell on her face
and on her dress which was white

in this moment she recognized
the face the person the woman

how can that be?

she rushed to embrace her

she could not help but fall on her knees
before the appearance which must be
—she concluded—the true candidate
the designated empress

Movement 4

she looked up at her: it was Ariane

my divine light, Ariane said to her
do not kneel before me because
an empress only kneels before God

i am no empress, she replied

i would not count on that
Ariane said and pulled her up
they embraced again

how did you get here? she asked

there is a secret door which
is known only to the consorts
it is knowledge of old

she pointed to a door
that stood slightly ajar
the faintest hint of air
was emanating from it

but why are you here?

because you have not
made up your mind

Ariane, i am not the empress
i am not in the legitimate line
the access to the crown is denied
the glass dome is firmly closed

my adored goddess, Ariane said
the mechanism does not release
if two people are in the room
the riddle is as easy as this

forgive me for being brief
we do not have much time

know then that the consorts
are completely one with you
they are always on your side
far beyond what the world
knows or could ever imagine

we have realized that you
are not fully decided and
thus we give you this option

pointing to the secrete passage
she continued

you can walk out of this door
and lead any life you want
be a servant to poor people
as you had intended to be
you can comfort any heart
that misses you, any soul
that longs for you

if this is your preference
then i will take the crown
and will rule in your place

i know all your thoughts
i am fully aligned with you
and by the grace of God
i am a flawless pearl too

in the splendor surrounding the empress
no one will know the difference
not today, not tomorrow
not till the end of time

not even the consorts will know
by their choice, by their resolve

we have agreed on this: all that
will happen is that one of them
a certain Ariane is missing

but she was just a pebble on
the shore like many others

a pebble?

yes a pebble! there are
many pebbles and many shores

Movement 4

in fact Ariane has left this morning
handing in her resignation

but consorts do not resign, she said
without the empress's approval

there is no empress, Ariane replied
with a smile, not yet

the other option is you take
the crown and become empress
in that case i walk out of that door

i will go into the world to give
my life in service of the poor
as you would have done

these are your two options
which one do you prefer?

but what do you want for yourself?
how can i affect your life so profoundly?

this, my divine light, is my choice
my choice is to give you this option
i live for you in one case or the other
living for you is fulfillment of my life

i do not understand...

do not worry for me, Ariane continued
i am a bodhisattva like you, i am only
here to make the choice symmetric
i am here to balance the equation
to conserve the energy of the universe
to keep the laws of nature invariant

and the mechanism would
release for either one of us?

yes, it does, it is very simple
the mechanism releases for a pure heart
for a bodhisattva who is in her last life

this then is our last life?

for her who takes the crown
it is her last life
for her who goes into the world
the path is unknown

while we do long for nirvana
both options are fine for us
do you concur?

yes, they are, i agree

suddenly they heard a faint sound
coming through the open door
outside it must be pouring
a heavy summer rain had started

still hesitating she asked
how can you be so devoted to me?

a silence ensued

then Ariane said, look into my eyes

she tried

this time it was hard for her

Ariane whispered, trace my eyebrows!

she gazed into her eyes
then she lifted her finger
to touch ever so slightly...
to trace...and then...yes oh yes!
i see...but how can this be?

she was transported back in time
two girls were running over meadows
one fell the other pulled her up

she could not control her ardor
both were beyond control now

the flow of emotions would have swept
them away in the whirls of spacetime
had they not held each other so strongly

they embraced one another
with all the life that was in them
their hearts were beating fervently

after a few minutes which seemed
to pass like an eternity of no words
Ariane was the first to compose herself

quick we have to act now!
what is your decision?

Ariane looked at her
fully focused, entirely resolved

her eyes narrow she said
remember your first decision
before the emissaries in the village
was a blank

but the second decision—now
—is for real—is forever

this decision is for real

what will it be?

7

in the cathedral the people saw
a figure appearing from the crypt
by their measure of time passing
she had been away a few minutes

it was dark in the church now
because it was pouring outside
the stellar crown on her head
reflected all available light and
even seemed to be a source of it

the solemn silence
induced a sense of awe
people did not know
if they were supposed
to look at her or not

some crossed themselves
and bowed their heads
others averted their gaze
after a brief glance

she simply stood there
looking at the people she loved

it seemed to her not only the crown
but also her dress emitted faint light

she decided this was too much
she raised her arms and lifted
the crown from her head

she turned around and walked
toward the altar of the church

she knelt down before the altar
and placed the crown on top of it

only he who sacrifices his life
in eternity is worthy of a crown
and his was one of thorns

Movement 4

she made a few steps back
knelt again before the altar
then turned to face the people

my beloved people
do not be misled
it is not a crown
that makes a queen

i do not need a crown
to be your queen
i am your queen and
you are my people

for this purpose
i came into the world

my life is offered
in service to you
i am your servant
you are my people

i will protect the weak
i will feed the hungry
i will comfort the mourning
i will uphold peace

my council is based on love
my rule on forgiveness

i reject every compromise
which calls into question
those two foundations

as for governance
all can appeal to me
but no one from me
responsibility is mine

for your good i demand
allegiance to my quest
obedience to my word

if you love me
you will obey me
my word is love

love illuminates the path
that leads us to God

if anything good arises
from my actions
it is a gift of God's grace
all glory belongs to God

in any moment
i am standing before God
with empty hands
a mere grain of sand
a particle of His creation

may the Lord help me
to be devoted to the task
He has asked me to fulfill

by the nature of love
His yoke is easy
His burden is light

there was silence

her simple words had reverberated
through the vastness of the cathedral
microphones had picked them up
and sent them out into the world

everyone in the audience was silent

but the silent thoughts which arose
in the cathedral of infinity were caught
by the books its building blocks

among them we found as follows

   ...she is a bodhisattva in her last life

... of purity and simplicity
that even the form herself
possesses only to lesser degree

... now she is visible to all
although she has been among us
invisible all the time

... the flawless self that resides
in every soul is only hidden by confusion

... composed of essence and existence
but not of accident and necessity

... goodness is no accidental property of her

... everyone could be she but no one is

... even time would rush to obey her

... she brings the prayers of people to God

... in her presence the Lord of Death
who is about to strike would hesitate

in the ceremony it had not been
stipulated for her to give a speech
she had established a new item
in the procedure which would be
followed for centuries to come

then she turned around
and knelt down before the altar

an ancient hymn started

again she prayed fervently
and her prayer was heard
and the answer was given

"because you have asked for this
i give you all you have asked for
and i will give you everything else
which you have not asked for..."

once the hymn had ceased
a bishop advanced toward her

next to him stood a prophet
who proclaimed in a loud voice
she is the one the Lord has chosen

then the bishop anointed her

first on her head
which brings forth
her loving thoughts

then on her eyes
which behold all the glory
and pain of the world

then on her mouth
which can utter no lie

then on her hands
which care for the
sick and the poor

he anointed her
before her people
successor of David
successor of Solomon
Queen of Sheba
Queen of queens
King of kings

Queen of all dominions
known and unknown

Empress and Augusta

he anointed her Queen
before her subjects

may the light of the Lord
forever shine upon you
may the goodness of the Lord
forever shine through you
and illuminate the world

8

a week later
loudspeakers announced
from every corner of the empire
in every town
in every village
at every crossroad
at remote outposts
in the furthest locations
of the inhabited
and uninhabited world:

the senate had made her a goddess

MOVEMENT 5

1

she washed the feet of the
suffering and the destitute
the ritual she had introduced
she performed with humility
people never knew it was she
those who thought they had
seen her refused to believe it

only in one fleeting moment
as their eyes met someone
identified her unequivocally
and she too knew she was
recognized beyond doubt

but as he watched her move
to the next person with eyes
lowered he resolved to hold
the secret in his heart forever

she visited attended by some
of her consorts and usually
unrecognizable among them
many services in the cathedral
she was moved by the events
she loved the hymns and chants
she knew the Latin texts

she worked in shelters and in
hospitals for the poor where
she was never recognized
she volunteered for work that
no one else was willing to do

2

i will tell you of my divine manifestations
i will mention only those which are prominent
for they are limitless

i am the true self in the heart of every creature
the beginning, middle, and end of their existence

of shining gods i am Vishnu
among lights i am the sun
of storm gods i am Marici
of mountains i am Meru

of scriptures i am the Sama Veda
of the lesser gods i am Indra
of the senses i am the mind
in living beings i am consciousness

among priests i am Brihaspati
among great sages i am Bhrigu
of vibrations i am the sound Om
of bodies of water i am the ocean

among trees i am the sacred fig
of musicians i am Citraratha
of perfected beings i am Kapila
of peaks i am the Himalayas

i am the flying horse produced
from the churning of the sea
i am the elephant with seven trunks
i am Surabhi the mother of all cows

i am the infinite, i am hospitality
i am the god of love, i am the sky
among the dispensers of law
i am Yama, the lord of death

Movement 5

*among animals i am the lion
among birds i am Garuda
among fishes i am the shark
among men i am the king*

*of rivers i am the Ganges
of purifiers i am the wind
among warriors i am Rama
of all measures i am time*

*of sciences i am self-knowledge
i am logic and conclusive truth
among seasons i am the spring*

*i am Brahma, creator of the universe
i am Lord Shiva who devours all
i am the source of everything that is to come*

*of feminine qualities i am fame, fortune,
fine speech, memory, intelligence, patience*

... go on! she said approvingly

*i am the gambling of the gambler
i am the splendor of the splendid
i am victory, i am adventure
i am the strength of the strong*

*among the Vrishnis i am Krishna
among the Pandavas i am Arjuna
among great thinkers i am Usana*

*i am morality, i am silence
i am the wisdom of the wise
i am the seed of all existence
nothing can be without me*

*but there is no end to my manifestations
i have revealed to you only a few of them*

*know that all beautiful and glorious creations
spring from a spark of my essence*

*know that i support the entire universe
with a fragment of my being*

she stopped reading, they were silent

...with a fragment of his being
her listener contemplated

and he never played the flute again?

3

your visitor has arrived

ask him to meet me in the olive grove

he is not very presentable, madam

i will look beyond his mien

he waited for her at the spot
deeply engaged in his thoughts
not perceiving her approach
when he finally noticed her
he bowed and she smiled

of men the wisest, she thought

he opened without ceremony
our next discourse was meant
to be on the nature of love

i am ready, she offered

will she be my instructress
in the art of love? he wondered

all people say love is a great god
they say love is beautiful and good
i assume you concur, he said

i do not, she replied

what? is love ugly and evil?

certainly not! why those extremes?
is that which is not beautiful ugly?
is that which is not good evil?

do you think that all those
who are not wise are ignorant?
or can you see a middle ground
between wise and ignorant?

what might that be? he asked

right opinion, she answered
right opinion could be unable
to give a clear reason and
therefore it is not knowledge
but it is not ignorance either
for ignorance cannot attain truth

similarly love occupies a middle ground
between good and evil, beauty and ugliness

but all admit love to be a great god
he countered

all who know? or all who do not know?
she asked patiently

just all, he answered

this cannot be right, my wise friend
since you and i do not hold this view

how come? he asked

it is so obvious, she answered
the gods have what they want
but love desires what she has not
love desires the good and the fair
of which she is in want

if love is not a god is she mortal?

love is neither mortal nor immortal
love is in between, she replied

love mediates between the provisional
and the absolute, between man and God
love brings the prayers of people to God
she reveals the wishes of God to people

the gods are not philosophers
they do not seek wisdom
because they are already wise

Movement 5

neither do the ignorant seek wisdom
ignorance has made them satisfied
hence they have no desire for that
of which they are not in want

philosophers are those people
who dwell between wise and ignorant

wisdom is beautiful, she continued
love is of the beautiful, love is a philosopher
a philosopher is a lover of wisdom
a being between wise and ignorant

but you call me wise, he said

i encourage my students, she joked

they walked uphill in the grove
that was planted by Athena

do not confuse love with the beloved
the latter is truly beautiful, she said

now he looked at her

yet the principle of love is another
as i am trying to teach you

o most revered woman, he said
mortal or goddess whoever you are
your words are wise and beautiful
what is the use of love to people?

if you love the beautiful what do you desire?
she inquired

i desire that the beautiful may be mine
he replied

what is the purpose of possession of beauty?

i do not know, he said

then let me replace "beauty" by "good"
if you love the good what do you desire?

the possession of the good, he replied

what do you gain by possessing the good?

happiness, he said, true and deep

this is a final answer, she remarked
since the purpose of life is to seek
happiness as we have established

the truth is that we love the good
we love the possession of the good
and not only the transient but the
everlasting possession of the good

then we agree that love is the desire
for everlasting possession of the good?

we agree, he admitted

if we agree this is the nature of love
then what is the manner of pursuit?
what are they doing who are in love?
what is the goal they have in view?

he looked at her and replied
if i knew i would not be here
to marvel at your wisdom

she laughed, then i will teach you

the object they have in view is
the birth of beauty in body or soul

the oracle requires an explanation, he said

love makes humans desire to procreate
which happens either in body or mind
love is not only for the possession
of beauty but also for its generation

please explain why "generation," he said

because for a mortal creature
generation is a step toward immortality

Movement 5

if love is of everlasting possession of the good
we desire immortality together with the good
wherefore love is of immortality

the mortal nature is seeking as far as possible
to be everlasting and immortal

this goal is attained by generation
because generation leaves behind
a new existence instead of an old

by generation the mortal body
partakes in a form of immortality

it is even true of knowledge
which changes over time
knowledge can be forgotten
and reclaimed by recollection

by substitution the worn out mortality
leaves another existence behind
in a process called evolution

unlike the divine which is always
the same and never another

the immense and bottomless love
which people have for their offspring
is for the sake of immortality

is that true?

you can be assured!

now think of the ambition of men
consider how they are stirred
by the love of immortal fame
they are ready to run risks
greater than they would have
for their own children

they undergo any sort of toil
and are ready even to die
for the sake of leaving behind
a name which shall be eternal

what vanity is a name! she thought

let me now introduce you
to even greater mysteries of love
i do my utmost to inform you
so please follow me if you can

she who proceeds on this journey
begins by visiting beautiful forms
first she loves one such form and
from that love spring fair thoughts
soon she perceives that beauty of
one form is akin to beauty of another

then if beauty of form in general
is her pursuit how foolish would
she be not to realize that beauty
in every form is the same beauty

when she gains this crucial insight
she will abate her exclusive love
of the one manifestation and
become a lover of beautiful forms

next she will realize that beauty
of the mind is more honorable
than beauty of the outward body

she will proceed to the sciences
and the art of geometry to study
their beauty with great eagerness

she will be drawn toward and
contemplate the sea of beauty
that now expands before her eyes

they had reached a spot which
offered an unhindered perspective

with a deep sigh she revealed
my good teacher used to call
this expanse the ocean of truth

Movement 5

who was your teacher?
he asked with a raised brow
his mind scrolling the list of
pre-socratics many of whom
he considered accidental

only a pebble... she said
lost on a distant shore

noticing the answer did not
resolve him from his worry
she added with a smile
he was my teacher in much
the same way as you are

this account pleased him
and he decided to let go

where were we? he asked

incidentally, she interjected
all learning is remembering

she looked at him sideways to gauge
his reaction but perceived none
oh well, those titans! she thought
one day it will be attributed to him

right, let us not digress, she said
but instead return to our discourse

she who is now equipped with tools
of science, geometry, or algebra...
again glancing at him... no reaction

... standing on the shore of the ocean
she will create fair and noble thoughts
of boundless love of unclouded wisdom
until on that shore she grows stronger

then a vision is revealed to her
of a single science which is
the idea of beauty everywhere

she who has come thus far
in her understanding of love
she will suddenly perceive
waves of wondrous beauty

and this my good friend
is the final cause of our toils

a nature which is everlasting
neither growing nor decaying
neither waxing nor waning

not fair in one view and foul in another
not fair at one time and foul at another
not fair to some and foul to others

but beauty absolute simple
everlasting without diminution
without increase without change

ascending in her pursuit of true love
she begins to see unchanging beauty

and now we are at the peak, she said

they had reached the very top
the panorama revealed the world
that was spread out before them

for you my friend it is the right path too
you can move or be moved by another
upward along the slopes of love

beginning with simple evident beauties
climbing for the sake of other beauties
using manifestations of beauty as steps

going from one to two, from two to many forms
from forms to practices, from practices to notions
until you arrive at the notion of absolute beauty

then at last you know the essence of beauty
which is also the essence of goodness

Movement 5

he looked at her and for once he was speechless

this, my dear friend, is the life above all others
which man ought to seek and want to live

life in contemplation of absolute beauty
which once seen would be regarded
as higher than anything material

you would not anymore long after
gold or fame or physical beauty
whose lure still distracts you

you would be content to see me at times
converse with me without food or drink
as i open your eyes to see divine beauty
and not mere shadows

divine beauty pure and unalloyed
is not clogged with the dust of mortality
not confounded by the vanities of humans

imagine holding converse with beauty
herself—simple, true and divine

remember how in that communion
—beholding beauty with the mind—
you will be enabled to bring forth
not images of beauty but realities
thereby generating true virtue and
becoming the friend of God

would that be an ignoble life?

he was astounded

this is much to grasp for one conversation
he said after some time

i trust in your memory, she laughed
but let me add one final remark and
please keep this last insight as well

we have used the word "possession"
we talked about possessing the good
this phrase could be misunderstood
it means "participating in the good"

the form reveals herself similar
to the workings of Divine grace
you cannot own her for yourself
loving her implies letting go of her

as you renounce selfish desire
you may long to be near her
but you cannot be one with her
you can never possess her

there is a mathematical analogy:
she is the limit of a sequence that
can be approached infinitely closely
but never reached—do you follow me?

he looked at her with blank countenance

she realized she was going too quickly

he said, thank you for your instruction
i request your permission to return soon
because many burning questions remain

your request is granted, my wise friend

as he walked away she wondered
did he register my last comment?

she watched his figure receding
downhill between the olive trees

i really appreciate and admire him
whether he will go down in history
as one or two remains to be seen
much wisdom will be built on them
many will subtract but few will add

then she turned around

Movement 5

on top of the hill was a temple
and next to it a small chapel
the latter was nearly invisible
as it was placed in the future

in front of the chapel stood
a consort holding a cloak
she walked toward the consort
who put the cloak on her

then she entered the chapel to pray
for him who was of a different time
and for many others because for her
all searching souls were contemporary

they were pebbles on the shore
who were waiting to be found

her resolve was not to lose a single one

4

in the palace rooms opened to the garden
instead of doors there were white linen sails
which slowly swayed in the breeze

the consorts weaved to instantiate texts
which were simple verses of wisdom
their threads moved swiftly in time

today they were generating
for a past without beginning
and for a future without end

they began by observing that
the truth that can be told
is not the eternal one
the name that can be voiced
is not the eternal one

of their queen they sang
she acts without doing
she teaches without speaking
she disperses confusion

she is a bottomless well
filled with infinite hope

she does not take sides
she heals sinners and saints

she is empty but inexhaustible
she saves countless worlds
she is infinite and eternal
she is present within us

she is detached from all things
therefore she is one with them
she knows that nothing is lacking
thus the world belongs to her

Movement 5

her generosity is like water
nourishing all without effort
yet being content in low places

in thinking she keeps to the simple
in conflict she is fair and generous
in governing she does not control

she loves and guides people
without imposing her will

she observes the world
she trusts her inner vision
she allows things to come
her heart is as open as the sky

worry and fear are phantoms
which arise from selfishness
they have no hold of her

she watches the turmoil of beings
and contemplates their return

when she governs her people
they are unaware that she rules
when her work is complete
they say we did it without her

because she is not proud
people can see her light
because she has nothing to prove
people can trust her words
because she is entirely unselfish
people can find themselves in her

however splendid the view
she rests calmly in herself
following the everlasting light
she receives the world in her arms

she does not force any issues
nor try to defeat opponents
she turns foes into friends

*because she is content within
she does not seek approval
because she accepts herself
the world embraces her*

*punishment she detests
forgiveness she upholds
loving kindness she practices*

*if you open the door for her
all things resound in harmony
the world becomes a paradise
all roaming people make peace
the law is written in their hearts*

*she is called humble and great
yet she is unaware of greatness
therefore she is truly great*

*when you see her the world is transformed
you become content with a simple life*

*she concerns herself with the depth
she is unencumbered by appearance*

*she dwells in reality and abandons illusion
her constant practice is humility*

*she views people with compassion
because she understands their longing*

*her greatest love seems restrained
her deepest wisdom appears silent*

*she makes use of solitude
she is one with the world*

*in her pursuit of knowledge
she grows stronger every month
in her practice of wisdom
she becomes more humble every day*

Movement 5

let her guide your life and you will find joy
let her enter your village and it will strive
let her fill the universe and it will sing

if you want to succeed follow her
use her light and discern the source

she considers critics who point out
her faults as kindhearted teachers
she thinks of enemies as shadows
which she has cast herself

she cares for other people
as a mother for her child

she remains humble and calm
humility gives her courage

her precious teaching is threefold:
compassion, patience, simplicity

she does not compete but she wins
she does not insist yet she is obeyed

she acts without expecting reward
she works without demanding credit
yet there is no limit to her love

evil cannot enter her heart

the consorts' airy weaves
floated through the palace
which became a limitless library

5

and on Easter sunday?

he was not recognizable
not by his appearance
only by his words
only by the logos

...and he said to you?

yes......touch me not
do not retain me...

fragments carried by the wind
and the monk attending the garden
with infinite love and dedication
heard them but did not keep them

these words like many others
over his long years of service
entered his mind like the few
remaining thoughts of his own
which still came as imperfections
but more and more rarely now
only to be let gone into time

MOVEMENT 6

1

it was a twilight scene
his senses were fading

fibers connecting him
to the stream of temporality
were severed one by one

he drifted in and out
of the material world
that was still present to him

suddenly the door opened
in a flash of light and hope
he recognized her at once
as we know people in dreams

both moment and eternity
with her were in him now

when she entered the room
she saw it was not too late

the program had triggered
for him the deep wonder
of a life lived not missed

she entered via his senses
but not only through them
because she was in him
as knowledge of the absolute
resides within us always

a subdued alarm went off
the people who came into
the room looked at her
as if asking for a decision

slowly she shook her head
and lowered her eyes
they left dejected

she sat down by his side
it was all peace now
it was all accomplished
the struggle was over

she watched him fall asleep
wander in and out of dreams
that were still composed
of those fleeting experiences

peacefully he glided on the river
of that one-dimensional time

he would become aware of other
dimensions soon, she thought

then the sensation of being
dragged along would cease

when he woke up he had
recovered some strength

he had seen her in dreams
which had filled him with joy
and glimpses of other worlds

he had often woken up
to the certainty that
she was beside him
but it was only moving
from one dream to another

in the new dream
he was even more joyful
than in the one before
because the new dream
confirmed the previous one
a dream but itself a reality

now he was sure
she was not a dream
but a formalism of
unsurpassed beauty

Movement 6

revealing that which can occur
in temporal material variations
revealing that which does exist
in atemporal immaterial certainties

she was an oracle pronouncing truth
a transformation over deep structure

truth that remains truth forever
she was a platonic form

soon she would lead him
through the world of those forms
as she had led him through
the library of all books
and the museum of all art
that was devoted to her

she had led him through life

could he enter with her
that unchanging realm?

had he finally reached
the entrance of the cave
and was now gazing at
the world as it really was
and always will be?

did he see for the first time
without the veil of confusion?

he was blinded by the light
that emanated from her
for the room was entirely
in darkness otherwise

the room was the cave
while she was the exit

the cave mattered no more
only the exit drew his focus
she was the door to eternity

which form did she embody?
the ideas lie dense in their space
indexed by normal numbers
containing all libraries, all lives

there are uncountably many forms
some are so close to each other as
to be indistinguishable in the limit

are the lives dense in their space?
and the souls that propel them?
are there uncountably many souls?
are all souls of one substance?
are all lives of one essence?

she returned with a glass of water
she wanted him to taste once more
the purity which transported all life

evolution unfolded in living water

can you crystallize platonic forms
that are dissolved in the water of life?
can you separate them physically
from the primordial ocean?

is there an algorithm in neurons
that leads to knowledge of them?
do cells have knowledge of her?

can a molecular process occurring
in the brain ever know a form?
or can only a form know another?

she is the form of unconfused existence
she had lifted her veil long ago

she had rejected all aspects
of selfishness one after the other
in a vast trajectory of maturation
until her payoff was that of others

the real payoff of others
not the confounded one
distorted by selfishness

Movement 6

if her payoff were that of others
then his would be included in it too

but he could not be wholly with her
unless his payoff was that of others
unless his payoff was hers entirely

only if their payoffs coincided
could they be fully together

if you fuse with one soul
then you fuse with God

once you are dead
—the thought of death
was far from him now—
you fuse with all souls

loving is like dying
dying to selfishness, dying to sin

now he realized
what it meant to be with her

he only needed to succeed
participating in her completely
he had to open the door from within

this door was his exit from the cave
he was the village, he was the cathedral
she was the orphan, she was the empress

if his payoff were that of all others
then they were truly together

in the crypt was another woman
whose payoff was entirely hers
who was ready to live for her
who participated in her fully

the two women in the print
were distinct yet indistinguishable

she had to be asked twice
first by the people and
then by the consorts

her answer in the village was
for the temporal material
her answer to the consorts
for the atemporal immaterial

the consorts are platonic forms
that know her fully
they are dense around her
she disappears among them

true power is not from people
true power is from God

power exerted by people
who are not in love with God
leads to suffering, limits life
and induces destruction

natural law springs forth
from the underlying reality
everyone can appeal to her
no one can appeal from her

here it was again—she was the judge
the good herself casts judgment

her answer in the crypt was clear
because her choice is forever
there is only one path to the light

she does not go back on her word
because she is timeless consistency
she knew that this life was her last

as his eyes were failing he could see

he turned to her and wondered
how was it that you knew so much
in all of our conversations?

Movement 6

sometimes it seemed you asked me
because you wanted to learn facts
but then you knew the answer anyway
did you ask me as teacher or student?

she looked at him and in her eyes
was all the love of the world

everything that is offered to me
with a sincere and loving heart
is illuminated by me and thus
known to me, she answered

her words flowed affectionately
and generated a warm placidity
in her voice was infinite kindness

every object made with love
every painting
every sculpture
every line of poetry
every composition of music
every simple meal
every sincere action
every good deed
sometimes mere fragments
attempts at something
attempts of reconciliation
even failed attempts
goals reached or missed
scientific experiments
calculations, games
studies of mathematics
a sunrise, a sunset
a bed of flowers
a golden tree of life
a single hand clapping
waking up on Easter sunday
all of this is illuminated by me

her words reached him
slowly he processed them

he realized he stood without proficiency
at the very beginning of something new

is life not beautiful?

illuminated was the key
in what she had said
illuminated! of course!

the Form of the Good
illuminates all other forms

did they not call her "light"
and even "divine light"?

i asked questions for your benefit
and for mine, she continued
i listened to your thoughts
i weighed your productions
i received your offerings of love

i delighted in our conversations
and through them i learned
how you saw the world

this was my objective as a student
i was both student and teacher

i followed your expositions
with a burning heart

for some of the questions
i knew answers others had given
but i wanted to know yours

not only absolute knowledge is
of interest to me but attempts
generated by searching minds

i seek to illuminate the hopes
and dreams of temporality

Movement 6

i desire to learn from people
their personal recognition of God
their individual spring of love

the love that is produced
by the creation is the union
of those individual attempts

this union is valuable to me
not only the intersection

each human life produces a unique
perspective that is inextinguishable
it is written down in the number
which accompanies the trajectory
of this one particular unfolding
each life is to be known and loved

a single number for an entire run
of a material universe? he asked

it suffices, she replied, as you know

then she was quiet again
and she was looking at him
with immense compassion

she sensed there was
physical pain in him
but largely subdued

she wished there were
a candle in the room
though she found none

she heard one burning
but it was her body
which burned to light

for how much longer
could she sustain this?

he slept again

she thought of Moses
who was found by a river
but died on a mountain
in the presence of God

in him was the image
of a winding river along
which his boat moved
in a crimson evening sun

the oar dove in and out
of the water without noise
the river was a sparkle
of gold and light with each
curve leading to a new
revelation, a new truth

truth is a property
that all true statements
and all true moments
have in common

a true moment is the realization
of being with her forever

the river was his refuge
from a world he increasingly
failed to understand
he was usually alone there
because the roads traveled
by others were orthogonal

natives had called the river the one
where grass grows at the bottom
a lover of wisdom had seen the nests
of the fish in the transparent water

in his thoughts she was with him
on the river that meandered
peacefully through time
the river was a symbol for
another one flowing to God

Movement 6

the universe was an expanding stream
of matter and energy sprinkled with isles
of consciousness that were floating along

he woke up

she continued

and know this: the way you have
experienced me everyone can

does this make you happy?
she asked looking into his eyes

very much so! he replied

i knew it would

the answer you gave long ago
at the street corner was the correct one
you made the right choice

i thought there were no choices, he said
there is only one path that leads to God

you are right again, she replied

she was silent

... a burning heart
had she missed him too?

he noticed the book which she held

is it this book? he asked
is it the book we brought with us
from the library long ago?

she looked at him

are we on the last few pages?

i am afraid we are, she answered
her smile was one of strength and regret

how does it end? are we dying in it?
or do we find a way out of the book?
out of the library and into the world?

we do find a way out, she said
this book leads us out of the library
you, me, the reader, all people
but the continuation is up to us

the book is neither beginning nor end
it is in the middle of the trajectory

but there is no coincidence here
because i picked a particular book
from the shelf of eternity

and this book is my present to you
in choosing it i did not play dice

now it was quiet around them
the late afternoon was suffused
by evanescent autumn light

it was cold outside
aimless leaves made the wind
while the trees were bare

colors had evaporated
accents had ceased

she walked to the window
looked out over the garden
there was a single rose left
defying the absence of hue

suddenly she felt lonely
and entirely heartbroken

again he gathered strength and said
then i no longer ask you who are you
as i have done so often before
instead i ask you what are you?

Movement 6

the wind outside was audible
moving leaves and branches
a window fell shut abruptly
but without breaking glass

you are right, she said
this is the correct question
and the answer was always in your heart

which was the place where he was now
more than anywhere else, more than
at any previous moment in his life
and she was there together with him

she knew she was now
his one and only thought
his one and only dream
as it had been intended
from the very beginning

returning to the bed
she saw the soul hovering
over the frail body
which was worn out

the soul was still young
ageless and unchanging
it cared for the body
the soul was in love with
the material manifestation
it had guided over time

she sat down again
mild und leise...[16]

she heard the candle burning
she listened to him breathing

then once more a smile on his face
and he said, what is truth?

now her eyes filled with tears
yes! what is truth? as we were
walking uphill between vineyards

and He too was asked that question
but no answer was forthcoming, he said

it was a rhetorical question
no answer was expected, she replied

again after considerable time he said
i do have one last question
there is one remark you made
which puzzled me more than others

you said in that night
they all abandoned Him
but where were you?

she looked at him
and now it was for her
to be astonished

quietly she replied
i was there
i was ready to fight
i was alone
but i could have held up a legion

yet He looked at me
and it was clear to me
that His decision was otherwise

what He intended to do
was something far greater
than i could ever have conceived

2

next morning the room was empty
the windows were open to receive
the cold and fresh autumn air

outside the rose had disappeared
leaving a colorless gap in nature

sunlight fell into the room and
onto the bed which was an altar

a young nurse made the bed
she had come here recently
to offer her life in serving others
she was from an orphanage

she had looked after the patient
in those last few weeks
she wondered why no one
had ever come to visit him
but at the same time she knew
that he had not died alone

she worked swiftly and gracefully
there was a tear in her eye

3

history's judgment
of her reign was uniform

she led them with
unwavering authority
as someone who knew
the varying compositions
of space and of matter
as someone who saw
through the confines
of temporal existence
as someone who was
beyond any confusion
induced by selfishness

historians point out that
strictly speaking she never
demanded obedience
but always received it

she rejected every compromise
that called into question the form
which it was her mission to uphold

as the supreme judge in her realm
she was not judgmental at all

she refrained from punishment
she was ready to forgive and
grant new chances to everyone
who applied to her in earnest

it was her sacred duty
to heal victims and culprits
since both carried wounds
of either body or soul

Movement 6

she comforted the weeping
she uplifted the broken
she fed the hungry

she mended a world
that had been tormented
by hate and greed for millennia

she had no conception of sin
she treated all people alike
irrespective of the path they
had taken before reaching
the circle of her light

everyone who comprehended
a mere fragment of her being
was forever transformed

she knew it was enough
if people saw the same God
in every person

if she enabled them to do so
her quest was complete and
everything else would follow

her supremacy was never challenged
her priestly virtues never questioned

under her rule peace flourished
extreme poverty ended
education of heart and mind
was made available to all

the earthly habitat was
preserved from destruction

she told people their primary
responsibility was to look after
each other and after the planet
which had brought them about

people fell in love with God
people fell in love with earth
people fell in love with her
and with each other

following her leading light
people became less greedy
selfishness turned unattractive
forgiveness replaced revenge

unconditional cooperation
became stable prompting
new mathematical theories
that were to her satisfaction

for herself she refused
any personal property
she considered material
wealth a distraction

always calm and composed
always loving and kind
she pushed her body
to the very limits
of physical endurance
and in secret far beyond

she concealed her exhaustion
even from those who were
closest to her on a daily basis

she let the consorts read
her wishes only at times
of her own choosing
as she had the ability
to withdraw into deep
meditation at any moment

she loved all people passionately
she saw what was good in everyone
she sincerely cared for them

Movement 6

her heart was always on fire
a fire that consumed her over the years
and brought her down in the end

on her deathbed—to everyone's
astonishment—she was tormented
by dark worries and bitter despair

she concluded that
she had failed before God
she had not done enough
to align this world with His love
she had not worked hard enough
to bring people to Him
she had not until now
participated in His suffering
she had failed her mission

some voices suggested
but absent real justification
there was a regret in her life
which she had never overcome

finally when the painful struggle was over
her body which was mortal after all
was laid into a small tomb
between the two grand ones
in the place she had singled out long ago

by her last orders the only inscription
it carried were the letters of her name

EPILOGUE

walking downhill between vineyards
they were talking about the future
they were happy in the moment
and made plans for tomorrow

opulent autumn had come quickly
mornings and evenings were cold
winds swept over harvested fields
trees displayed magnificent colors

there was a tranquility of moods
a sense of farewell ending summer
fogs hovering over pastures of elves
untouched waters in riparian forests

the sun was deep now
it had the chroma of incensed gold

the shadows of the hills
behind which she would set
had almost reached them

they walked downhill
they were unconcerned
and talked about the future

he looked back and thought
there on the top of the hills
the sun will remain much longer

then he voiced her name
and she turned toward him

her brief glance recalled
memories from long ago
of their first summer when
he could not hold her gaze

Beethoven walked here, he said
and Mahler heading to rehearsals

Movement 6

i know, she replied kindly
while touching his arm
you are telling me this
every time we pass here

what is the concert tonight?
he asked trying to recover

Das Lied von der Erde

i am looking forward to it

me too, very much

are we in a hurry?

no not yet, she replied

their friends considered
them a good couple
their children had grown
they never had arguments

their conversations continued
but they were no longer deep
they were never on fire

he still had dreams
but they were rarely of her

his book about her published
long ago was his life's work
yet no one knew or suspected
that she was the inspiration

cynics rather declared she had
a helping hand in writing it

he considered that statement
to be true in more ways than
one but did not talk about it
some people had suggested
he should write another book
but he thought it was not in him

on the ridge the receding sun
set the autumn leaves ablaze

he had noticed the warmth in her voice
she was at his side now and so was God
noises from the city arose and mingled
with fragrance of the descending evening
winegrowers were gathering their harvest

the city received them into her arms
as the nature around them grew cold
a warm cozy room waited for them
he was looking forward to the cups
of steaming tea she would prepare

he did not worry about the future
he had always lived in the present
for him the moment was eternal
all astonishing and all embracing

long ago she was omnipresent
in his thoughts and his longings
she was the pivot of all his ideas
and the destination of his journeys

then she was always there
when he was most happy
other times were irrelevant
he had lived for those moments

their lives had seen turmoil
he had received some wounds
but never experienced anger
nor ever blamed others

it was her influence

the first summer was vivid in him now
when he was unable to hold her gaze
when his ardent love consumed him
and yet reduced him to utter silence

true awe is silent, she had once said

then one afternoon she came unexpectedly
her hair was wet, raindrops were on her face
she had been running through a downpour
she was breathing heavily

she was unusually agitated and very moved

he could not fathom what had happened
he always considered it impertinent to ask
her for explanations—he never did

i am fine, she smiled, really fine
catching her breath

he followed her into the room

i am here to close the deal, she said
in a low voice whose timbre would
have been interpreted as seductive
by anyone who had experience

he had none

she turned and looked into his eyes

he had not grasped
the meaning of her words
she was uncertain
if he had perceived them

she realized her sudden appearance
had overloaded his sensory input

she sat down on the sofa
he wanted to sit on a chair
opposite her or even better
on the floor below her
if that was permitted

she pointed to her side
she started a conversation
her hand was in her hair
but this time it was not
the topic of the discourse
that engaged her mind

over the next few minutes
she moved closer to him
and closer

all of a sudden he became
aware of her resolve

he covered his face

he noticed the fragrance of her skin
which was still damp but drying fast

before then only the souls embraced
but what was to come now?

he never understood the purpose
of the materialistic experience
ideas and souls were all to him

we are bodies too, she explained

instantiation is a platonic form
is real, did you never fathom this?

not before now, he replied

as they walked downhill between
vineyards the sun set for them

there was a house for sale

now they took interest
in those mundane matters
but not then when only
the foxes had their holes

sitting on the sofa facing him
her hands slowly reached for his

hands that had worked the soil
that had washed the floors
that had fed the hungry
that comforted the mourning
that cared for the sick and the dying

hands therefore that held in them
all the riches of the world

the tips of their fingers touched
negotiating uncertainty

if i profane... he thought
good pilgrim!... she replied

her other hand moved forward
her fingers tracing his eyebrows
barely touching, then his forehead

did she make the sign of the cross?

i claim you before God...

who are you?

i know that i know nothing
she replied

as they descended some stairs
they were suddenly cold
he put his hands in his pockets
she buttoned up her coat
then fastened her shawl
which had come loose

she had bought it long ago
on one of their trips
on a serene terrace
facing a southern ocean
when a cool evening breeze
had suddenly engulfed her

on the sofa she looked at him
he was trembling

her face was so very near
her breath entered him
their lips almost touched

in the last moment
he turned away, sank to the floor

he now knelt before her and
buried his face in her hands

no mortal is worthy of you

i am no goddess, she answered

i am not worthy of you

yes you are

your soul is fundamentally good
your soul always trusts
always hopes, always perseveres
your soul may reach for mine

he saw that she had forgotten
to take off her shoes
already kneeling before her
he began to remove them

am i worthy to untie the straps
of your sandals? he joked—to gain time

she smiled

he noticed that her shoes were
rather unusual golden sandals

i have never seen you wearing those, he said

they are second hand, she explained

proceeding on the path downhill
which both Beethoven and Mahler had
traversed although at different times
they noticed that nature was inflamed
and that the leaves were burning
in the receding sunlight

they passed a cemetery

a cemetery in the autumn
is this the end of summer?

is dying difficult? she wondered

he thought of their first summer
the unending light that emanated
from her, the light of the one and
true morning star which never sets

it depends, he answered
it is unpredictable

        in the room with her shoes removed
        she had also glided to the floor
        they sat leaning against the sofa
        closely embracing each other
        she listened to his heart beat

        she realized she had to give him
        more time, probably infinite time

        there was eternity before them
        but not as a sequence of moments

        instantiated matter feeds on time

        he was breathing the air she exhaled

        are you a mirage? he asked

        i am real, she answered
        everything else is a mirage

        she pointed to the observable universe
        that was a small sphere around them
        finite numbers vanish before infinity

        no mortal is worthy of you
        he repeated on the verge
        of bursting into tears

        with great tenderness
        she aligned his face a second time

        look at me she said
        i am a mere mortal
        kiss what is mortal!

as they descended further
in the fading autumn light
he thought of their first walk
over those hills where they
had mused about philosophy

the beautiful events of Easter
then floating in the warm water
and sitting at the staircase

the nightly visits to that cafe
in the center of the city she loved

that summer meant everything to him

>   in the room
>   there was a dance
>   of lights and shadows

>   her skin was warm and dry
>   her eyes were closed

they reached the end station of the street car
they had just missed one
they waited for the next one
when it arrived he opened the door for her

may i?

you may

>   she trembled
>   as they found each other
>   but in them was no trembling
>   only certainty
>   as two souls fused
>   into a single one
>   was only love
>   an unconditional
>   everlasting
>   absolute promise
>   even beyond death

and in the moment afterwards
when the last ecstatic scream
of the now one soul had dissipated

when there was only silence
and the silence was the memory
of what was or what could have been
the memory of a life lived or missed
the path of a world saved or lost

when she pressed herself
against him with all her love
and all her fragility
he was absolutely sure
he would never die

ENDNOTES

Beyond uses *italics* to indicate quotes. Sources and inspirations—unless given in the text—are as follows:

MOVEMENT 1

Chapter 1: Mahler, *Symphony Number 2, Resurrection*; Goethe, *Werther, Faust*; Shakespeare, *Romeo and Juliet*.
Chapter 2: Goethe, *Werther*, "Letter of 10 May," translation by R. D. Boylan (Project Gutenberg) with modifications by author.
Chapter 3: *The Easter Proclamation (Exsultet)*, with modifications by author.
Chapter 5: Goethe, *Faust*.
Chapters 7 & 8: Doderer, *Die Strudlhofstiege*.

MOVEMENT 2

Chapter 1: *Bhagavad Gita*, translations by A. C. Bhaktivedanta Swami Prabhupada and by Eknath Easwaran, with modifications by author.
Chapter 3: Augustine, *Confessions*.
Chapter 4: inspired by *Dhammapada*, translation by Eknath Easwaran.
Chapter 6: *Gilgamesh*; Vergil, *Aeneid*; Homer, *Iliad*.
Chapter 8: Yoshiro Tamura, *Japanese Buddhism*, Kosei Publishing 1967, first English edition, 2000; quotes attributed to Saicho, Genshin; *Lotus Sutra*.

MOVEMENT 3

Chapter 1: Goethe, *Faust*.

MOVEMENT 4

Chapter 4: Schiller, *Maria Stuart, Don Carlos*, Eminescu.
Chapter 6: Goethe, *Faust*; William Blake; Bible: Isaiah, 1 Corinthians, Revelation, Gospel of John.
Chapter 7: Bible: 1 Kings.

MOVEMENT 5

Chapter 2: *Bhagavad Gita*; translations by A. C. Bhaktivedanta Swami Prabhupada and by Eknath Easwaran, with modifications by author.
Chapter 3: following Socrates's speech in Plato's *Symposium*, translation by Benjamin Jowett, with modifications by author.
Chapter 4: inspired by the *Tao Te Ching* of Lao-tzu.

MOVEMENT 6

Chapter 1: Wagner, *Tristan und Isolde*.

TRANSLATIONS OF NON-ENGLISH QUOTES

1 when the entire world around me rests in my soul...

2 *Verweile doch, du bist so schön*
   stay a while, you are so beautiful

3 Lamb of God that takest away the sins of the world

4 grey dear friend is all theory
   but green is life's golden tree

5 they do not hear the following songs
   the souls to whom i sang my first

6 Faust exclaimed, i know a lot
   but i want to know everything!
   Mephisto countered, much i do
   know but omniscient i am not

7 my adored beloved

8 (unusual for:) do not remind me of the past

9 (quite literally:)
   when the leaves are lying on the steps
   autumn breathes from the old stairs
   what has walked over them long ago
   moon (light) in which two held each other
   light steps and heavy strides
   the mossy vase in the center
   endures years between wars

   much has disappeared—to our grief
   and the most beautiful is of shortest duration

10 (her) hair given to winds to scatter it

11 heed well the heart is a betrayer
   but nothing deceives the eye of flame
   which looks within...

12 the god of this earth (meaning the king)
   must learn to renounce

13 remain! you are so beautiful!
   the trace of my days on earth
   cannot disappear in eons

Endnotes

14 you will be like God knowing good and evil

15 Hail, hail true Body,
born of the Virgin Mary,
having truly suffered, sacrificed
on the cross for mankind
From whose pierced side
water and blood flowed
Be for us a sweet foretaste
in the trial of death!
in the trial of death!

16 calm and quiet

ABOUT THE AUTHOR

MARTIN NOWAK is Professor of Mathematics and Biology at Harvard University. He is a leading researcher in the areas of theoretical and evolutionary biology. He has proposed that cooperation is the third fundamental principle of evolution, alongside mutation and selection. His work has helped to create fields such as evolutionary dynamics, virus dynamics, mathematical oncology, and evolution of cooperation. He has published more than 500 papers and four books. For many years, Martin has also been working in the domain of Science and Religion. Before coming to Harvard in 2003, he held professorships at the University of Oxford and the Institute for Advanced Study in Princeton. In 2015 he received the honorary degree of Doctor of Humane Letters from the Dominican School of Philosophy & Theology at Berkeley. He is Roman Catholic.

Printed in Great Britain
by Amazon